THE SUPERHERO SOUL

Praise for *The Superhero Soul*

'If simple steps can create big differences and introspection can lead to transformation, Dilip Bathija's *The Superhero Soul* is a masterpiece of a journey that would help millions transform their lives.'

– Dr. Satasuryaa Sharma
(Chairman, National School of Leadership)

'*The Superhero Soul* is a must-have for anyone on the journey to build a better life. It is written in lucid luminous language and is full of moist interesting stories, anecdotes and is peppered with inspiring quotes. It gives simple steps to improve your life which are totally practical and easy to follow. This is a small but power packed book.'

– Nitin Sanker
(CEO, Middle Earth HR, Asia's largest and World's 7th Largest HR Training Company)

'Amidst our daily chores and the repetitive cycles of joy and despair, we tend to forget our greatness. *The Superhero Soul* re-introduces us to the greatness within ourself to bring revolutionary results.'

– Khurshed Batliwala
(Spiritual Master, Social Reformer and Educator)

'Dilip's style draws its power from its sheer simplicity and the raw power of eternal truth. A beautiful reminder of our *Superhero Soul* and our limitless immense possibilities. It is difficult to be unaffected by it. Thanks Dilip, for such a gem.'

– Nandita Sanker
(India's No.1 Emotional Freedom Technique Practitioner)

'*The Superhero Soul* is a great book to get unstuck. It helps you tap into your inner strength and gives you the energy to make a difference.'

– Jithin C. Nedumala
(CEO, Make A Difference Foundation)

'*The Superhero Soul* is a warm hearted journey to our most intimate source. It offers us not just a map, but the hat and shoes, not just inspiration, but the actual tools that enable us to get 'here' and to authentically express the brightness of our being in each moment of life. Enjoy this adventure.'

– Nithya Shanti
(Spiritual teacher, Educator, aka The 21st century Monk)

'*The Superhero Soul* elevates you to a higher level in life.'

– Dinesh Ghodke
(Spiritual Master, Social Reformer and Educator)

THE SUPERHERO SOUL

QUEST FOR INSPIRATION, HAPPINESS, SUCCESS AND GREATNESS

DILIP BATHIJA

BLOOMSBURY
NEW DELHI • LONDON • OXFORD • NEW YORK • SYDNEY

First Published, 2015

BLOOMSBURY PUBLISHING INDIA PVT. LTD.
New Delhi London Oxford New York Sydney

ISBN: 978-93-85936-01-2
ISBN: 978-93-84898-91-5 (CAD/USD)

10 9 8 7 6 5 4 3 2 1

Published by Bloomsbury Publishing India Pvt. Ltd.
DDA Complex LSC, Building No. 4, 2nd Floor
Pocket 6 & 7, Sector C
Vasant Kunj, New Delhi 110070

Laser Typeset by FORTUNE GRAPHICS, Naraina, New Delhi

Printed and bound in India by Thomson Press India Ltd.

The quote/s of the following individuals have been used with prior permission from their respective agents/authorities:

Winston S. Churchill
Permission obtained from Curtis Brown Group Ltd., London on behalf of the Estate of Sir Winston Churchill (www.curtisbrown.com).

Napoleon Hill
Permission obtained from The Napoleon Hill Foundation (www.naphill.org).

Dr. A.P.J. Abdul Kalam
Permission obtained from the office of Dr. A.P.J. Abdul Kalam.

Doris Lessing
Permission obtained from Jonathan Clowes Ltd., Literary Agents to Doris Lessing (www.jonathanclowes.co.uk).

Sri Sri Ravi Shankar
Permission obtained from the CEO of The Art of Living Magazine (www.artofliving.org).

Note: The aforementioned individuals or their authorities do not endorse third party products.

Dedicated to you

The Superhero Soul

Contents

Acknowledgements

From the core of my being, I would like to thank every person who has touched my life in one form or another, for embracing me, teaching me, inspiring me, enlightening me, and shaping me. Thank you so much, Superheroes!

Especial gratitude and love to:

My family – mom, dad, grandpa, brothers and sisters, and my beloved grandma, who taught me love and my very first life-lesson. I cannot be thankful enough for what you have given me all your life and cannot speak enough for what you mean to me. Thank you for tolerating my craziness and everything else.

All the teachers, gurus and mentors who for centuries have and continue to lead the way of humanity, spreading wisdom and compassion and advocating self-mastery, I bow down to you in immense respect and gratitude. I will always be your student and your biggest fan.

Another Superhero, Manisha Jain, thank you so much for your magical editing. You make me look like a pro writer. You're awesome!

The Superhero domain experts, who took time out of their crazy schedule to read this book and share their reviews, I thank you and show my deepest respect to you.

My Superhero friend, Shantanu Mandal, for beautifully

crafting the illustrations for *The Superhero Soul*, which left everyone awestruck.

My publisher, the late Suresh Gopal, at Bloomsbury India. I pay my homage to you and thank you so much for your guidance and for believing in *The Superhero Soul*. You will be dearly missed.

The entire team of Superheroes at the Bloomsbury office, for your dedicated and exquisite efforts on *The Superhero Soul*. This piece would not look the way it does without you.

My dearest friends, reading *The Superhero Soul* in different places around the world, you teach me the true meaning of friendship. Thank you, for your moral support and encouragement. I feel privileged to share this bond with you.

My special well-wisher who brings out the best in me, the word 'Thank you' is not enough. I celebrate your presence each moment of my life.

The seeker, and my inspiration. What is noteworthy is your overwhelming enthusiasm about *The Superhero Soul* since its inception. I thank you for being a part of this journey, immersed in self-transformation and self-mastery. *The Superhero Soul* now belongs to you.

1

The Source Within

Introduction

> *The most powerful weapon on earth is the human soul on fire.*
>
> **Ferdinand Foch**
> (1851–1929, Military theorist)

For as long as we can recall, human beings are known for betterment. There is an undying belief in human beings that, at times, astounds and lights up the world. It makes those times extraordinary. History is a witness to it.

This power in humans is synonymous with the cliché on the walls of their hearts that says 'We settle only in the betterment.' During the Stone Age, our ancestors bettered to create fire and hunt animals. Then, they bettered to make clothes to wear and created shelter for safety. In the agricultural age, they bettered to get better quality of food and better living conditions. In the industrial age, they continued to be better to get oil and coal in the global trade.

Even today, the betterment continues. After all, the meaning of life is growth – advancement. Even as you read this book, you are striving to be better off in your life. However, the majority of betterment throughout history has been and continues to be the contribution of a chosen few Superheroes who changed the time completely and who broke the shackles of our mental limitations of what was or is considered possible.

We are all blessed with the same physical composition – two

hands, two eyes, two legs, perfect organ systems, etc. Yet while millions struggle, a handful of them fulfil their dream.

The truth is that these few people brought out the best in themselves. They brought out the Superhero from within to become Superheroes. They looked in a direction that others failed to see and began their journey. Now you can too!

This book will help you make that journey and re-introduce you to the Superhero inside you, which will rewrite history and change the legacy of humankind forever. It will help you rise up like the rising sun. It will bring magic into your life by moulding your character. It will enrich your personal life while empowering your professional life. It will harmonize you at all the levels – physical, mental, and spiritual. Each part of this book will take you a step closer to becoming a better, more successful, happier, and the most contented person than you were originally meant to be. It will lead you to your bliss. If you make this book your coach, your friend, and your well-wisher, it will unleash the Superhero in you.

It all starts here.

You Are All-knowing

> *God is an unutterable sigh, planted in the depths of the soul.*
>
> – **Jean Paul** (1763–1825, Writer)

There is nothing new that you're going to learn from this book. There is nothing new that I can teach you because there is nothing that I know that you don't already know! This book will help you discover and realize those powers, and find the source that lies within you. All that is there in this book is already within you. You have just forgotten about it.

You are not aware of your capabilities because you have lost contact with the source of your capabilities. You have been locked in a cage of complexities and negative perceptions. Unused items, over a period of time, get covered with dust. Similarly, the source within has been covered by the complexities and negative perceptions of the modern world. But, it does not mean that the source does not exist. And you will find it when you believe that it exists.

An aeroplane exists for you because you are aware that it exists. Electricity exists for you because you acknowledge its existence. Whatever you think exists, exists because you are aware of its existence. But to the tribal people living in a deep forest, a washing machine does not exist nor does your computer. No internet, no dishwasher, no contact lenses, etc., because they are not aware of their existence. But this does not mean that they don't exist. Even a fish contained within the limits of a small glass bowl eventually dies sooner than in an ocean. Similarly, when you don't become aware of the powers within, you limit yourself. The essence of living a life dies within the limits. Be that which you truly are – limitless!

> *You have to grow from the inside out. None can teach you, none can make you spiritual. There is no other teacher but your own soul.*
>
> **– Swami Vivekananda**
> (1863–1902, Monk)

2

Journey to the Source

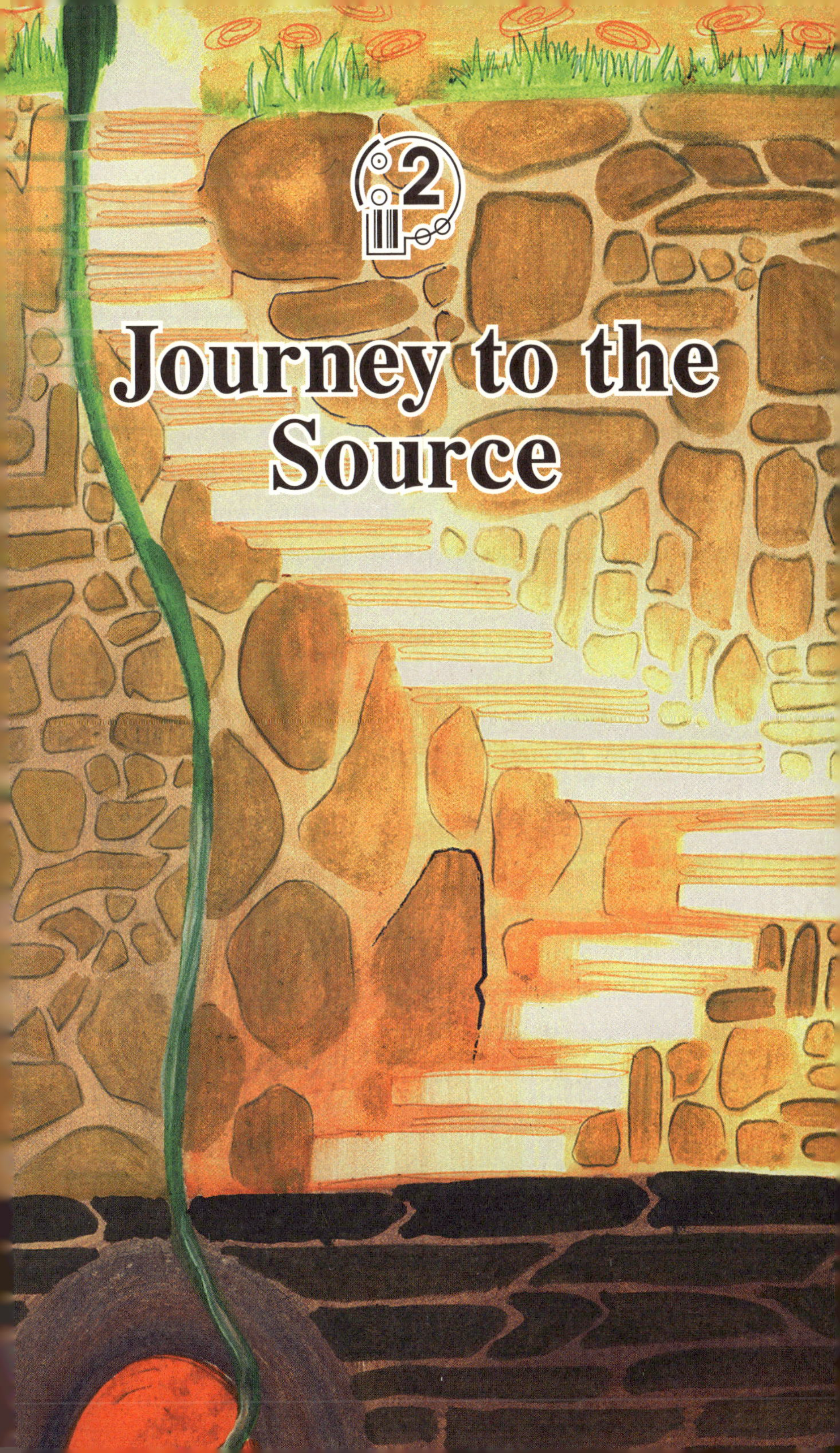

Bury the Past

To make your journey to betterment, to a brighter future, you cannot carry the oft-beaten baggage of sadness from the past into the future. Bury the past right now, and seize the present. Don't judge anyone based on who they were or what they did. Don't evaluate your future on the basis of your past. Your future is based on your present moment and what you do with it now. Remember that no matter what happened yesterday, it cannot destroy your today unless you give it the power to do so. So, stop being the prisoner of your past and start being the architect of your future.

> *We are made wise not by the recollection of our past, but by the responsibility for our future.*
>
> – **George Bernard Shaw**
> (1856–1950, Playwright)

All the wrong experiences that made you bitter – let them go. All the hardships you had to undergo – let them go. All the wrongs done to you – let them go. All the heartbreaks you had – let them go. All of it – just let it go. Letting go of the old things that dull your life makes space for new things to brighten it up.

One of the best ways to bury the past is to forgive and forget.

'To err is human but to forgive is divine.' Forgive yourself and all those who make you a prisoner of your past. Forgiveness frees you from your past. But, if you can't forgive and forget, at least, don't sit and crib about your past. It clearly doesn't do any good for you. Instead, make the pain one of your biggest strengths.

Muhammad Ali's life was filled with struggle and adversity, but he managed to rise above each challenge. In 1954 in Louisville, Kentucky, 12-year-old Ali's bike was stolen while he and a friend were at the Columbia auditorium. Young Ali found a cop in a gym, and boiling with youthful rage, told him that he was going to 'whup' whoever stole his bike. The cop admonished, 'you better learn to box first.' In no time, Ali had his first bout, and his first win. What Muhammad Ali did was stand up, become stronger, and fight. A stolen bike was the key to the beginning of the Muhammad Ali's story. He didn't cry over what happened. He converted his pain into his strength.

You can either stand up or be a victim of your circumstances. You can't be both. Either forgive and forget or just bring it on! Make the pain your strength and put on your A-game. You've got to do one of these. You can't just do nothing.

Stop Comparing

You are meant to make your journey happily. But one of the chief sources of unhappiness and jealousy is comparison. Comparison robs us of the essence of all we have. Some people compare themselves to others from their first waking moment. 'Gosh, I have to wake up at six in the morning to get ready for my work, and look at the neighbours, they're still sleeping.' This continues on their way to office as well, 'Look at all those rich people, driving their fancy cars to work, while I have to use public transportation.' In the office, when one of their colleagues submits his project report, 'O my God, I didn't expect him to submit this early, and I am still only halfway through.' When your colleagues sit and have a casual talk about the possibility of a promotion, you say to yourself 'I started working in this office after him. He has been working here long before me. So my promotion will also be after his.'

> *How much time he gains who does not look to see what his neighbor says or does or thinks, but only at what he does himself, to make it just and holy.*
>
> – **Marcus Aurelius**
> (121 AD – 180 AD, Roman emperor)

One of the most destructive things you can do to yourself is spend time thinking how successful your friends, relatives, colleagues, and acquaintances are becoming. How many times have you let your heart sink on seeing others finding their perfect soulmate? How many times has your heart dipped on seeing others buy their dream home, their dream car, go on their dream holiday?

You have two options at your disposal. One is to cry out loud, complain that life isn't fair, those who have a dream life are just lucky, they are selfish and mean, and whatever else will comfort you momentarily. The second option at your disposal is to stop comparing yourself to other people and realize that crying and whining won't move a feather in your life. Instead of creating that drama in your life, you can choose to take the necessary actions to get your dream life.

You are a limitless being. But, by comparing yourself to others, you take the limits of others. Hence, no matter whom you compare yourself with, you will always feel inferior to them because they are their own original and you are just trying to duplicate them. There is no fun or joy in being a duplicate. If you compare yourself to others, you will feel low and unhappy most of the time. And when you compare your success with that of the others, at the most you will achieve what they have achieved. Not beyond. If you keep limits, you will never know what it is to be limitless. If you always are in the known, you will never know the power of the unknown.

So many people spend most years of their life comparing themselves to others. They end up living somebody else's life with only disastrous results in their professional, personal, financial, and spiritual conditions. They eventually realize that the only life they could have lived was their own.

If you stop comparing yourself to others, you'll discover what is important to you and get to work on your goals and not theirs. You will understand how high your aim is. You will invest your energy in your work and not drain it by jealousy and worthless comparisons.

Focus on your footsteps, not others. Learn to master yourself, not others. You are priceless, limitless, and a source of an unparalleled greatness and a wonder in yourself. You don't need anybody's approval. Begin your journey knowing this.

3
Finding the Source

Finding Your Passion and Purpose

Your purpose will guide you to your source. The purpose of life is to have a life of purpose. But how do you find your purpose? One of the simplest ways to find your own purpose in life is by listening to *your* instincts, finding *your* passion. There are countless people who will tell you who they think you should be, starting from your parents to strangers. But it is your life. Claim it.

Imagine the world we would be living in if Edison became a violinist, Beethoven became a scientist, Einstein became a professional boxer, Michael Jordan became a wildlife expert, or Steve Irwin played basketball. The world is different because they followed *their own* passion, *their own* bliss.

Now, how do you find out what you are passionate about? Ask yourself what you can do for six to eight hours a day, five days a week, without worrying how much money you can make from it yet having fun while doing it. That's passion.

Sir Ben Kingsley continues to act in movies. He is 70 years old. He doesn't have to act to make money and he doesn't have to act to get respect. He already has ample of both. He continues because of his passion for acting. Warren Buffet continues to work at the age of 83, not for money or things, but because of his passion for investing. Steve Irwin lost his life chasing his passion. Today, people celebrate his life. It was his passion for being a wildlife expert that made him great.

> *To begin, you must know what drives you. Simply because not knowing will mean that you can never begin to satisfy yourself. What does money mean to someone who hungers for love?*
>
> – **Napoleon Hill**
> (1883–1970, Writer)

You may be interested in a thousand things. That's great! But if you want to be successful, you have to be passionate about something!

Passion makes you come alive. A wife comes alive when she does something for her loving husband. A child comes alive when he sees his mother. A football player comes alive when he is on the field playing. A scientist comes alive when he is experimenting in his lab. A philosopher comes alive when he contemplates. An entrepreneur comes alive when he goes that extra mile. A playback singer comes alive when he works with a piece of music. A soldier comes alive when he serves his country. What makes you come alive?

Our life can be only as great as our purpose. As Goethe said 'A useless life is an early death.'

Make Lists

There is an incredible power in writing. Begin with making a 'why' list, 'goal' list, 'fear' list, etc. But before we begin making lists, it is very important to understand the power in making lists.

It all goes back to a story about a young man, who was the son of a horse trainer, who would go from stable to stable, racetrack to racetrack, farm to farm, and ranch to ranch, training horses. But one day, a task given to him by his teacher, to write what he wanted to be and do when he grew up, changed his life forever. This young man grew up to be Monty Roberts, who achieved every goal he wrote on the paper during his high school!

More than 95% people, who make lists and write their goals, achieve them. But sadly, less than 5% people of the world's population make lists.

Use a diary that you will carry always with you. Make your own 'to do' lists. Write down every single idea you have, no matter how big or small. Mark off every task completed, every goal achieved, every fear overcome.

'Why' List

Unless we know why we are doing what we're doing, any obstacle or challenge can break us. To really rise above them, we must have a strong and determined 'why?' We must have a strong purpose behind what we are doing.

Let us imagine that you and I are going on a vacation. We have chosen to take the train as our means of transportation. In the middle of our journey, I take you near the door of our train coach and ask you to break the glass door and jump out of the running train. Will you jump? This time I *request* you to jump. Now, will you jump? No. You'll simply ask me, 'Why should I jump when there is no reason to jump?'

Now, let us again imagine the same situation all over again, that you and I are going on a vacation. We have chosen to take the train as our means of transportation. In the middle of our journey, I take you near the door of our train coach and ask you to break the glass door and jump out of the running train. However, this time I tell you that the engine of the train has caught fire and that it may explode any time now. The train is about to topple off the tracks and self-destruct. This is your only chance of survival. This is the only time to save our lives. Jump. Now will you jump? Yes!

What changed your mind this time? I gave you the 'why.' You jump only when you have a reason to jump off. Similarly, only when you know why you have to do a 9-to-5 job can you fulfil its purpose and eventually live the purpose of your life. So take your diary, make the first list: the 'why' list. Write down the reasons why you do what you do. Remember: your 'why' is more important than your 'how.' 'Why to do' makes 'How to do' possible.

Goal List

> *If a man knows not to which port he sails, no wind is favorable.*
>
> **– Lucius Annaeus Seneca**
> (4 BC–65 AD, Philosopher and statesman)

What good is a life when you don't know what to do with it? What good is a life when you don't know its purpose and don't set yourself a mission and a vision?

> *Yes, I am a dreamer, for a dreamer is one who can find his way by moonlight, and see the dawn before the rest of the world.*
>
> **– Oscar Wilde**
> (1854–1900, Writer and poet)

Many people don't achieve what they want because it always remains as a wish. Wishes can be 'I want to go on a world tour,' 'I want to buy a car,' 'I want to buy a house,' 'I want to study abroad,' etc. Turn your wish into your goal. Be crystal clear about which car you'd like to buy, the colour, model, and the cost of it. Is your dream house a duplex or a mansion or perhaps a castle or a palace? Which university would you like to study at abroad, and at which intake? You have to believe in it, set a deadline, and convert your wish into your goal.

Make 500 goals for yourself. You can start with 25 and keep adding more with time. You can categorize your goals into short term, middle term, and long term. Short term can range anything from one day to six months, middle term can range from six months to three years, and long term can range from three to seven years.

Include personal goals, professional goals, recreational goals, and spiritual goals. Your personal goals may include your dream of owning a home, your professional goals are your career goals, your recreational goals may include your next holiday destination, physical goals like reducing weight, etc. Your spiritual goals may include undertaking a meditation course, visiting the holy places, being of service to others, philanthropic activities, etc.

Don't write: 'I want to buy a car' or 'I want to buy a BMW 5 series car.' That's not good enough. If I ask you, after a year if you have bought your dream car, you'd still tell me that you want to buy a car. Even after five years, you'll tell me that you want to buy a car. Your want always remains a want. Your car always remains in the future. Write your goals in present tense. Write the description, the experience, and the specification.

For example: 'I am so happy and grateful that today, December 31, 2014 (date on which you wish to buy), *I am* buying my brand new BMW 5 series car, model 530D, metallic black in colour and worth $70,000.' 'It is such a joy to drive my dream car, cruising through the smooth roads at 150 miles per hour with greenery and mountains on either side of the road. This is a dream come true and I am absolutely loving it!'

Even the poorest can afford nothing but an opportunity to play in the field of dreams.

Dream Big

> *Dream lofty dreams, and as you dream, so shall you become. Your vision is the promise of what you shall*

one day be; your ideal is the prophecy of what you shall at last unveil.

– James Allen
(1864–1912, Philosopher and writer)

If your aim is to buy a used scooter, you cannot buy a brand new Ferrari. But if you aim for a Ferrari, you can buy a used scooter.

If you aim to buy a duplex, you cannot buy a palace. But if you aim for a palace, you can buy a duplex.

If you study to score 50% marks in your exam, can you get 90%? No! But if you study to score 90% marks, you can get 50%.

If I tell you to come to my home tomorrow morning at 3 am, so I could give you same candy, will you wake up and come? No! But if I tell you to come to my home at 3 am, so I could take you for a ride in my brand new Ferrari California, you would!

Big thinking inspires you to take big action! A Ferrari could do what a candy could not.

The greater danger for most of us lies not in setting our aim too high and falling short; but in setting our aim too low, and achieving our mark.

– Michelangelo
(1475–1564, Sculptor,
Engineer of the High Renaissance)

How much effort would you put in to buy a used scooter? And how much effort would you put in to buy a brand new Ferrari?

How much effort would you put in to buy a duplex? And how much effort would you put in to buy a palace?

How much effort would you put in to get 50% marks? And how much effort would you put in to score a perfect 100%?

If you are poor, can you donate a million dollars to find a cure for cancer? No! But if you're wealthy, you can! Only when you have more, you can share more.

Aim for the sky. Reach for the stars and nothing lower. Stretch yourself and reach for the brass ring. If your goals are mediocre, you will always find yourself in competition. But once you dream really big, you will suddenly find yourself all alone. That is where the brass ring lies.

> *All who have accomplished great things have had a great aim; have fixed their gaze on a goal which was high, one which sometimes seemed impossible.*
>
> – **Orison Swett Marden**
> (1850–1924, Spiritual writer in the New Thought Movement)

Gain Knowledge

> *It is impossible for a man to begin to learn what he thinks he knows.*
>
> – **Epictetus**
> (55 AD–135 AD, Philosopher)

To be able to learn and grow, one needs to first unlearn all that one knows. And when you let go of all that you are and all that you know, you can embrace the unknown. Only then, can you truly learn and be what you want to be. One cannot feed a person who is not hungry. Similarly, one cannot teach someone who is not willing to learn.

But when you are ready to unlearn what is not required and learn only what is required, you can make that journey from who you are to who you want to be, from where you are to where you want to be. When you are not ready to learn, even the wisest of sages cannot teach you. But when you become a student, the teacher appears. Then you'll learn from a person, an insect, a thing, a movie, a song, a book, a mistake, nature, from everyone, everything, and everywhere!

Learning Is the Pre-requisite

Even though you may be someone with a predisposition to become what you want to be, you must still learn the skills of it. Someone with the predisposition to engineer a product must learn the basics in his domain. Someone with the predisposition to sing must learn the basics of music.

> *The man who graduates today and stops learning tomorrow is uneducated the day after.*
>
> – **Newton Diehl Baker**
> (1871–1937, Politician)

Involve Yourself

No matter how many books one may read on swimming, one cannot be called a swimmer. No matter how many books one may read on how to drive a car, one cannot be called a driver. To become a swimmer, one has to get into the water and apply what he learnt from the book. To become a driver, one has to position himself in the driver's seat and drive the car. Look at some of the dropout entrepreneurs, some dropped out of a business school and are billionaire entrepreneurs today. They understood that no matter how much they read in a business school, they'll eventually learn far more by doing it.

> *Tell me and I forget. Teach me and I remember. Involve me and I learn.*
>
> **– Benjamin Franklin**
> (1706–1790, Inventor, politician, and the founding father of the United States)

Be a Domain Expert

> *An investment in knowledge pays the best interest.*
>
> **– Benjamin Franklin**
> (1706–1790, Inventor, politician, and the founding father of the United States)

If you want to be successful, you have no option but to be a domain expert. A mechanical engineer must know how the engine works, what are the components of an engine, what are the manufacturing techniques, what are the various types of mechanisms, etc. A civil engineer must know what beams and columns are, what are the various structures, how to draft a blueprint, how to design the structure of the building using a software, etc.

Look at Tom Hanks, Shahrukh Khan, Leonardo DiCaprio, Meryl Streep and tell me that they aren't domain experts in acting. Look at Barrack Obama, Ban ki-Moon, Dalai Lama, Pope Francis and tell me they aren't domain experts in being global leaders.

Look at Bill Gates, Narayana Murthy, Jeff Bezos, the late Steve Jobs, Mark Zuckerberg, Jerry Yang, Larry Ellison and tell me they aren't domain experts in technology. Look at Warren Buffett and tell me he isn't a domain expert in investing.

Look at Giorgio Armani, Mario Prada, Guccio Gucci and tell me they aren't domain experts in making luxury products. Look at Gordon Ramsay and tell me he isn't a domain expert in being a chef.

All these people are experts in their field!

One person cannot master all things. But one person can master some things. Choose what is it that you'd like to do as a career, or just as a hobby. Then get down to learning it, mastering it. Be the epitome of success in whatever you choose to do. There is no fun in being an amateur. Be a professional, be someone beyond the regular. You must be a domain expert and choose to achieve your goals. There is no shortcut.

Expand Your Horizons

If you are a salesman, attend quarterly sales report meetings. Attend motivational seminars to boost your sales. If you're an employee, interact with the senior management. Don't just be a regular employee, be a great employee. Assume the company as your own and strive to improve. Present ideas that will help the company grow. If you're self-employed, find ways to expand your business. Meet investors and potential clients that could help you in making your leap. Network with people to expand your horizons, feel the strength you never felt before. There isn't any fun in being ordinary. Be a domain expert.

The Universe Is Mobile!

Every minute, every moment is changing, evolving. But many people do not change. They remain stagnant in space and time. I am 24 years old and I regularly ask myself, 'Am I 24 years old or 4 days old?' I keep myself updated with the latest news and information in my area of interests. Ask yourself, are you as old as your age or are you a couple of days old? When was the last time you updated yourself with valuable information that brings progress to your life? Like the cell phone that does not get updated gets outdated, if you are not updated, you're outdated. Update yourself. Change yourself.

Knowledge Abolishes Darkness

When you're updated, you feel confident and it boosts your self-esteem. When was the last time you really felt confident about yourself?

We feel confident when we wear new clothes and enter a party. We feel confident when we are recognized or awarded. We feel confident when we get a driver's license. We feel confident when we are able to share the right knowledge with others. When we learn and do new things, we feel confident. Whenever we learn and grow and change, we feel confident!

But if we do not learn and grow and change, we remain outdated models. Think about this. What do you ask for when you go to a Nike, Reebok, or Adidas store? Do you ask for the latest models of shoes or the outdated models?

What do you ask for when you go to the mobile phone store? You ask for the latest model!

Develop a passion for learning. If you do, you will never cease to grow. It is highly important to keep learning in the domain that interests you. That way you will always have a sense of youthfulness within you and can teach others at your home and workplace and might even end up teaching another teacher.

Fear List

Fear defeats more people than any other one thing in the world.

– Ralph Waldo Emerson
(1803–1882, Essayist, poet, and transcendentalist)

All of us are already successful on the inside. We just haven't seen it on the outside. Our fears prevent our brilliance to radiate on the outside. Each one of us is a diamond, truly priceless. And just as the diamond has to let go of all the unwanted particles that surround it in order to shine, in order to become priceless, we have to let go of all our fears.

Our success has been covered by our own false shadows of fears. When the fears are eliminated, we see that we are already successful. And the first step in eliminating our fears is identifying them.

What is it that you fear? Make a list and write down your fears. Once you've written down your fears, compare them with your goals. See that there is more to be excited about your success than be afraid of your fears. The next step is to do what you fear. You have more strengths than your weaknesses.

Your fears only give you the opportunity to bring out the Superhero in you. Think about this: one of the primary reasons why people don't succeed is because they think more about their fears than their dreams. Don't let the fear of failure overpower the excitement of success. The timid soul that fears inside can reveal the Superhero outside when challenged! Destiny awaits those who surrender their fears to chase their dreams.

> *Jump, take that flight, and build your wings on the way down.*
>
> **– Dilip Bathija**

Fear is a natural part of starting down a new path. Don't go *away* from fear, go *to* it.

Fear is All in the Mind

Think about it. How many of your fears have ever come true? Research has shown that more than 80% of our worries or fears never come true.

Be Fearless

Many people fail not because of fear but because of lack of understanding about fear and lack of ability in dealing with fear.

Rise above your fears. You can rise above only when you know your fears – your limits. And when you rise above your fears, you rise above your limits. You push the bar higher. You set your standards higher. Your fears can be the goldmine of your growth. But our most common fears come from things that do not exist, or have not happened or will never happen. They are simply the results of negative thinking patterns that have been inculcated in you by external influences. And these negative influences affect you only because you allow yourself to be affected.

If you want to live fearlessly, drop the unnecessary baggage of what other people think of you, and the fear of failing and embarrassment. And when you feel light after you have dropped the baggage, take action. Identify and conquer your fears.

Finding and acting on your fears takes you into the unknown. But when you don't work on your fears, you will always lie in the known. You will always be within the boundaries of your fears. And that's not good. That's bad.

Act

An ounce of action is worth a ton of theory.

– Ralph Waldo Emerson
(1803–1882, Essayist, poet, and transcendentalist)

The only way you're ever going to turn your weaknesses into your strengths is by doing some activity. Activity cures fears. Many people talk a lot about their goals, their passions, about what they are willing to do to make them happen, and so on. But when you look closely, you will see that what they say and what they do is not aligned. There are also people who keep giving advice to everyone around them but never really apply the same advice to their own selves and never really amount to anything. They don't practice what they preach. They don't walk their talk.

It is not enough to just dream. You have to go out there and make your dream a reality. You see, it does no good to an artist if he *only* contemplates a picture. He must take the brush and paint his masterpiece. It does no good to a swimmer if he *only* sees himself winning the Olympic gold medal. He has to get down in the pool and swim. It does no good to a student if he *only* thinks of studying for his exam. He must study for it. It does no good to an army commander if he *only* thinks of giving the winning command to his army. He must give it. It does no good to a hungry man if a plate of food is served in front of him and he *only* thinks of eating. He must use his hands and eat. You can either think of doing it or you can just do it! Just positive thinking will not give you success. Just the will to win won't bring you success. But positive thinking, combined with inspired action, brings success.

Your audio and video must match up. Your passion and action must match up too. Winners know that actions inspire, not words. It took serious and dedicated action for Roger Bannister to break the four-minute barrier. But it was his action that enabled him to create the world record. It was this action of his that inspired other runners to break the barrier. And the world rewards you for your actions. Not your words. And in these times, do more – get more, do less – get lost!

A human is not human at all until he acts like one. What is

a Superhero if he doesn't act like one? What would be the legacy of all the Superheroes we know if they only spoke and never did anything?

Action and Inspired Action

There is a huge difference between action and inspired action. Just like there is a ton of difference between doing things simply for the sake of doing and doing things for the passion of getting it done. In action, followers are hatched. But in inspired action, leaders are born. They don't wait until the order is given to prepare. They are already prepared. They go the extra mile. When an employee gives his company more than what is expected of him, when he goes that extra mile, and when you see him having fun with it, you know he is doing inspired action. He is a leader and the future of the company. In action, work is done for the sake of being done, for the sake of executing the order. In inspired action, there is an adrenaline rush, there is a wanting to jump into action, there is excitement, eagerness, and positive energy.

Your action proves your passion! Action and passion go hand in hand; one is incomplete without the other. You may have gained the knowledge. But the application of knowledge is powerful.

> *Act as if failure is impossible and your success will be assured. Wipe out every thought of not achieving your objectives, whether they are material or spiritual.*
>
> **– Anonymous**

Starting Makes the Difference

Twenty years from now you will be more disappointed by the things you didn't do than by the ones you did do. So throw off the bowlines. Sail away from the safe harbor. Catch the trade winds in your sails. Explore. Dream. Discover.

– Mark Twain
(1835–1910, Writer and humorist)

Don't wait. No matter how risky it seems, no matter how tough it seems, no matter how complicated it seems, start. In every game there is winning and there is losing, but if you're afraid of losing and decide not to play the game, you've already lost! Unless you start, you're never going to make it, but if you start, at least you have a shot.

Many people think they can't better their lives because they don't have more. Hence they can't do more and eventually can't be more. But it's the other way around. We have to first be more, so we can do more, and have more. The change must first come from inside, only then can we see the change outside. You don't need anything to start. You just need to start.

Start by doing what's necessary; then do what's possible, and suddenly you're doing the impossible.

– St. Francis of Assisi
(1182–1226, Catholic friar and preacher)

Don't be a mere thinker, also be a great doer. The world is shaped by doers, not by mere thinkers. Just like a potter has to use his hands to give shape to his work, doers start and get into action. Their actions speak louder than their words.

Life is all about taking chances. If there are no risks, there are no rewards. It terrifies us all, but where will we ever go in life if we don't take a chance? You can make the choice right now to take a chance and be glad later that you did it. Or would you rather at the end of your life say 'I wish I had taken a chance back then?'

If you want a better life, start taking chances now! Take calculated risks! The number one thing that separates the winners from the crowd is that the former took more calculated risks. It is very easy to play safe. But it just doesn't take you anywhere.

> *Don't be too timid and squeamish about your actions. All life is an experiment. The more experiments you make the better.*
>
> – **Ralph Waldo Emerson**
> (1803–1882, Essayist, poet, and transcendentalist)

You can always live in one place for the rest of your life because you know the place and think it's safe. You can always work at the same job you hate because it is safe. You can put all your money in a savings account because it is safe. Or, you can take a chance, live in your dream city, go after your dream job, seek better investments, get out of bad relationships, and go after the things you really want in life!

Sometimes taking one big risk can be all that you need to do change your life forever. When we don't take risks, life becomes dull and monotonous. A life spent in regret is more painful than a life lived in failure. So, keep taking chances and keep learning from them. Life becomes more entertaining and more worthwhile when we take risks rather than just sitting on the sidelines and watching others pass by. And if you don't know where to start from, start from anywhere. But start now!

The beginning is the most important part of the work.

– **Plato** (427 BC–347 BC,
Philosopher and mathematician)

4

Protecting the Source

The Silver Lining

In the middle of difficulty, lies opportunity.

– Albert Einstein
(1879–1955, Nobel Prize winning Physicist)

Seeing the silver lining is protecting the source. If it rains, don't be sad. Be happy that your grass is getting watered without effort. If an old building collapses in a storm, don't be sad, be happy that a new building will take its place. If you don't get a cab, don't be sad, be happy that you can walk and you won't have to pay for the gym. If a meeting is cancelled, don't be sad, be happy that you've got more time to perfect your presentation. It is up to you to keep your cool and look for the silver lining.

You cannot measure a man by his failures. You must know what use he makes of them. What did they mean to him, what did he get out of them.

– Orison Swett Marden
(1850–1924, Spiritual author in the New Thought Movement)

You can either think doubt and taste failure or think victory and taste success. The choice is yours. When you choose to look at the positivity and learn from every situation, and not choose to react or panic by looking at the dull side of it, you'll find happiness everywhere and in everything. Then you protect yourself from going back to being the deteriorated version of yourself.

Criticism

The greatest prison that people live in is the fear of what other people think. Don't let others' opinion of you matter more than what you think of yourself. This will hinder your growth and greatly diminish your happiness. Ignore the critics and follow your dreams. Throughout history, there have been those crazy ones who have been criticized, labelled 'mad'.

Mahatma Gandhi, the Wright brothers, Abraham Lincoln, Edison, Walt Disney, Albert Einstein – all were criticized and labelled 'mad' for their ideas and pursuits.

> *First they ignore you, then they laugh at you, then they fight you, then you win.*
>
> – **Mahatma Gandhi**
> (1869–1948, Father of the nation)

If people label you 'mad', I think it's quite an achievement. You are now in the same page with Gandhi, the Wright brothers, Lincoln, Edison, Walt Disney, Einstein, etc. The people who label you 'mad' don't know that 'mad' simply means 'Making A Difference!' So, the next time someone calls you 'mad,' take that as a compliment and thank them.

The World Does not See What You Want to be

En route to achieving your goal, the world might just not want to support or help you. By world, I mean family, friends, your competitors, and anyone who is in the dark, ignorant to the Superhero within. They might as well try to stop you. The reason is simple. If you have a stomach-ache, then nobody but you feel the pain. Others can only sympathize you. So are your dreams and your visions. They can only be felt and realized by you. See the brightness within you, and not the darkness that surrounds you.

> *Great spirits have always encountered violent opposition from mediocre minds.*
>
> – **Albert Einstein**
> (1879–1955, Nobel Prize winning Physicist)

When you feel like a lone ranger, remember that there are only a few of our kind of Superheroes in every part of the world. But if you are not afraid of the voice inside you, you won't be afraid of the voices outside you.

Be a Sandalwood Tree

It is said that a sandalwood tree is surrounded by poisonous snakes. Yet the tree is not affected by the poison. It embodies too great a sweetness that is unchanged even in the face of danger. You can relate to those moments of your life when you were really happy and suddenly someone tells you something or some incident happens and it crushes the smile on your face and brings you crashing down. And this incident repeats with many of us, almost every day. It is like a shadow that never leaves, firmly holding onto us. But only until you realize that it is not the shadow that is holding onto you, but you holding on to the shadow. Keep your positivity amidst negativity. Next time when something like that happens, remind yourself of the sandalwood tree.

> *Whenever anyone has offended me, I try to raise my soul so high that the offense cannot reach it.*
>
> – **Rene Descartes**
> (1596–1650, Philosopher, mathematician, and writer)

If you can look for the positive in every situation, it's good; you make a simultaneous learning process. But if you can't, just walk away! No social obligation is more important than protecting yourself from negativity.

When good things begin rolling, make sure you close all the doors and windows so that no negativity enters and steals your precious moments. Exhibit unshakeable confidence, resilience, and faith in yourself. That way, no one or nothing can deter you from being happy or pursuing your strongest desires.

> *Entire water of the sea can't sink a ship unless it gets inside the ship. Similarly, negativity of the world can't put you down unless you allow it to get inside you.*
>
> – **Anonymous**

The Sine Waves

Life can be pretty much like the sine waves. There are ups and downs. If it goes up, enjoy the moment as you rise high and learn what needs to be done as you rise high. If it is going down, learn again. And be rest assured that it will rise high again. You must remember that you never learn while going up what you learn while going down. If you go up, you win, if you go down, you learn. Hard times are learning times.

In 1898, Professor Samuel Langley, one of the world's most respected scientists, was given $50,000 to build his dream – a flying machine which the world came out to see. The great aerodrome collapsed and Langley gave up, dying a broken man. Years later, two high school dropouts had the same dream. Without any funding or support, they pursued their dream. They crashed too, only until a winter's day in December 1903 when they flew their $1000 homemade flying machine. The Wright brothers pursued their dream where Professor Langley gave up. Do not let your situation be an excuse for your failure, but a reason to succeed!

The Unusual Business Meeting

I was in a leadership conference meet where a heart-touching story was shared. There was a sales representative who was very passionate about the products he was selling and the company he represented. One day, he had to meet one of his important clients through whom he was expecting his big break. He met the client in a park where they discussed their business. Before leaving, the client asked him why they hadn't discussed it over at the representative's place as a house was being demolished by a bulldozer in front of the park, causing noise pollution. The representative replied to his client saying that the house that was being demolished in front of the park was his house. The client, in shock, asked him what he was doing there with him while he was supposed to save his house. The representative smiled and replied 'I was building a new one.'

Indeed, smiling in the face of adversity is not a vice but a victory!

So you see, you're not the first and the only human being on this planet going through difficulties. Get a life! Every great being who has walked upon our planet has had his set of ups and downs.

Look around you – your parents, teachers, friends, neighbours, their children, their parents, their relatives, your relatives, their neighbours – everyone has problems. So, why are you whining about your problems?

The problem is not the problem. The problem is that we don't want to face them. It's not the problem that is the problem, but our reaction to it.

> *Fix your course to a star and you will navigate any storm.*
>
> **– Leonardo Da Vinci**
> (1452–1519, Renaissance polymath)

You are bigger than any adversity you'll ever know. I promise. Every challenge makes or breaks you whether you use it or lose it! If you can't run, walk. If you can't walk, crawl. Just don't quit. Keep learning and keep moving ahead!

Be courageous and say: 'Come what may, the show will go on!'

The Will to Win

It is not unusual that when there is action, there will be a reaction. It may start from a single person and result in an entire world trying to stop you from what you are doing. It is easy to put in words, but very difficult to go through it. It may weaken you sometimes and beat you down at times. But even if there is the feeblest voice in you that says 'I want that no matter what,' get up and try again. A Superhero is no braver than an ordinary man, but he is braver just few minutes longer. The road to every persistent action begins from the will. This simple formula changes everything:

Passionate positive thoughts + willingness to take charge of your life + inspired action = *Unbelievable results*

A will finds a way.

– Orison Swett Marden
(1850–1924, Spiritual writer in the
New Thought Movement)

I believe where there is a will, there are many ways, but you *must* first have the will. It took the will of Edison to give us the light bulb. It took the will of Nikola Tesla to give us the AC current supply and remote control. It took the will of Rockefeller to show us the power of a business model. It took the will of Jesus, a prophet, to spread the message of love and peace. It took the will of Mandela to abolish apartheid. It took the will of Bell to give us the telephone.

Nobody can lead if they lack the will. Nobody can invent if they lack the will. Nobody can be faithful in a relationship if they lack the will. You can't make people lead any more than you can make a horse drink once you've led it to the river. You cannot become better without the will to be better. Nobody improves by accident.

Stop giving power to your challenges. So many people live lives of quiet desperation because that's what they choose, that's what they accept. The ones who are on top didn't glide their way there. They too faced challenges, probably more than you, and probably they are facing them right now. They didn't give power to them, they just faced them with power invested in them. They gave power to the solution, not to the challenges.

Choose to be in love with the feeling of being determined, get addicted to it. What does a *Superhero* do when his challengers beat the will out of him? The Superhero rises up! In the midst of dismay, find that indomitable spirit in you.

Hope and Faith

According to Christianity, hope is considered to be one of the most important virtues that should be used by believers in church. Every religious and spiritual text in the world spreads the message of holding on to hope and faith in the heart.

Hope is the flame that keeps us going even in the face of uncertainty. Hope for the best of everything in your life. Hope that your perfect companion will show up. Hope that all the money you ever need is making its way to you. Hope that your dream job is waiting for you. Hope that your health is recovering with each passing day.

> *The soul shines with faith.*
>
> – **The Rig Veda**
> (Circa 1900 BC, Ancient Indian sacred texts)

Have faith in your hope. Faith is the very fibre of life. Without faith, human beings cannot achieve anything. If we observe all the Superheroes in this world, we find that they had faith in their hearts and souls. Your faith can be your Aladdin's genie. It can move mountains for you. It makes all things possible. It forms the foundation of every new journey.

Faith arises from the core of your Superhero soul, to which all things *are* possible. Faith keeps you focused on the destination and excited about the journey. Every great discovery in every field of the world has taken place only because of a virtue called faith. Faith moved Alexander to conquer the whole world, only to be known later as Alexander 'the Great.' Faith in humanity moved Mother Teresa to serve the ill, needy, and the underprivileged. Without faith, there would be no advancement in science or humanity.

Faith is the starting point of all accumulation of riches. It is the basis of all 'miracles,' and all mysteries which cannot be analyzed by the rules of science!

– **Napoleon Hill**
(1883–1970, Writer in the New Thought Movement)

It is the faith you have in yourself that you'll get a good job once you graduate. It is the faith you have in the pilot of a plane that he's a good enough pilot not to crash. It is the faith you have that you'll wake up the next morning that you plan the activities for it the night before. We all have faith in something in life. There is no one in this world who doesn't have faith. Faith is that part of your soul which cannot be removed. So, all you have to do now is to have faith in your good than in your bad. Tolstoy rightly remarked: faith is the force of life, the mother of success and with it, anything is possible! Develop the faith that you will be what you want to be and that it is inevitable, and that it is your destiny.

Faith is the nature of an undivided mind, an undivided consciousness.

– **Sri Sri Ravi Shankar**
(Born 1956, Humanitarian, spiritual leader, and ambassador of peace)

Understanding Success, Understanding Attitude

Age, Gender, and Location do not Matter

Some of the common misconceptions that many people believe in will be some of the biggest roadblocks on their path to success. 'I am too young to do that,' 'I am too old to do that,' 'I am from a poor background,' 'I do not have any support to do it,' and this and that. Your age, gender, and location are no match for the Superhero soul in you. It is ageless, knows no gender difference, and is powerful enough to shape anything you desire from any part of the world. Your family and social backgrounds do not exist for the Superhero soul in you. It is a pure creative force. So, miracles can be created by a two-year-old child and also by a 100-year-old person; by a person in London and a person in Alaska. We all, irrespective of our age, gender, location, colour, cast, or creed, are *Superheroes*!

When we spoke on this topic with Sreelakshmi Suresh, one of the youngest CEOs in the world, she said, 'I can recall a journalist who once asked me how I could be successful at such a young age, being a girl and that too in this country?' She added 'Age, sex, location – it does not matter at all. That's all there is to it. It just doesn't matter.'

Understand this: a young kid started uploading his songs on YouTube. He was discovered at the age of 14 by a talent manager and ever since there is no stopping to him. The kid went on to become Justin Bieber, one of the biggest sensations of the music world today.

This restaurant owner was well near the age of retirement when he invented his unique recipe. But due to the new highway construction that diverted the traffic miles away from his restaurant, his business was close to failing. Yet he believed that he could do it. He walked the long miles, pitching his unique recipe and was even knocked back 1009 times before someone decided to give him a chance to create what is now known as the highly successful food chain KFC. Colonel Harlan Sanders's age was well over 60 when he made it big with Kentucky Fried Chicken.

He was successful as an actor, yet he became the 40th American President only at the age of 70. During his tenure, President Ronald Reagan made drastic changes in economy to help increase economic growth. This even resulted in the coining of the term 'Reaganomics.'

If you really think about it, age is just a number, gender doesn't matter, and place is just another name.

These prodigies are an example to the world that age, gender, location, family, financial, and social backgrounds just don't matter to excel and be the epitome of success in your field.

No matter who you are, where you are, or how old you are, you have the power to say 'This is not how my story will be told!'

You Must Believe in Yourself

As soon as you trust yourself, you will know how to live.

– Johann Wolfgang von Goethe
(1749–1832, Writer and politician)

Believing in yourself is all about being sure that you are going to do whatever you want even if others are against you. Usually, when you decide to take a big challenge or to do something that people failed to do, you will find that everyone is pulling you down. Under the pressure of this criticism, some people start to doubt their own abilities and eventually give up. The few people who manage to believe in themselves and who continue moving along the path they've chosen are the ones who succeed.

Know your worth and *believe* that you are the most important person in the world. There is a universe of infinite potential in you.

Believe in Your Work

> *Believe that with your feelings and your work you are taking part in the greatest; the more strongly you cultivate this belief, the more will reality and the world go forth from it.*

– Rainer Maria Rilke
(1875–1926, Poet and novelist)

Do you believe in your work? Do you enjoy your work? Do you find it meaningful? Are you proudly able to describe your work to others or are you mumbling about it? If you are able to do so, then your work is making a positive impact in your life. But if you do not believe in what you do, it will bring no good to you. Find something that makes a positive difference in your life.

Believe in your work. Stand up for what you believe in. Preach it. No matter how new your business model is or how absurd your technology concept is. Nobody has the power to pull you down. So, don't bother about the crowd that criticizes. Imagine the world that'll be transformed. If you don't believe in yourself today, you will end up discarding your powers and you will have to accept whatever comes to you. Believe in yourself today. Others will eventually believe in you tomorrow.

The Amazing Power of Confidence

> *I learned this, at least, by my experiment: that if one advances confidently in the direction of his dreams, and endeavors to live the life which he has imagined, he will meet with a success unexpected in common hours.*
>
> **Henry David Thoreau**
> (1817–1862, Philosopher and leading transcendentalist)

Confidence comes when you have gained knowledge. And when you have gained knowledge, fear dispels. And where there is no fear, confidence blooms. Confidence grows when you think you can! Confidence comes when you are no longer afraid to make mistakes.

Imagine the time of your childhood when you were forever happy in your world. You would sing, dance, and let your heart out without any worry or fear. Had someone asked you to stand on a stage and address ten thousand people in front of you, you would have done it happily. But now that you have grown up, you are afraid to even go onto that stage. You feel nervous; you get stage fear, some people even faint considering the notion of getting on the stage.

Today, we are so afraid to make mistakes. And in that process, we stop trying. We stop experimenting with our lives. We lose the thrill of being alive.

What happened? If you have got yourself in this situation, so you can get yourself out of this too. Find those moments in you when you had unshakeable confidence. Get back that sparkle in your eye.

> *If you have no confidence in self, you are twice defeated in the race of life. With confidence, you have won even before you have started.*
>
> – **Marcus Tullius Cicero**
> (106 BC–43 BC, Philosopher, consul, and constitutionalist)

Where to Find This Confidence?

When I met a president of one of the leading companies of Asia, I asked him how he was successful both personally and professionally. With a smile he replied at once 'Because I think I can.' He added, 'Every morning I wake up and I affirm to myself "I can do it, I can do it, I can do it", over and over again for the next 30 minutes.'

> *Whether you think you can or think you can't; you're right.*
>
> – **Henry Ford**
> (1863–1947, Industrialist and founder of the Ford Motor Company)

Develop the habit of affirming to yourself that you have already got what you want from your life; that you have already become what you want to be. Because you truly are what you say you are.

Nothing is impossible to the Superhero in you. Say to yourself that you do not know what you can do. Because when you say that you know what you can do, you put a limit on what you can do. But when you say that you do not know what you can do, you become limitless, you can do anything. That is how the nature of the Superhero in you is, it is limitless. *It can* do anything!

Refuse to believe anyone who says you can't. All great men who were told 'you can't' went ahead and did it. Your life can be one of the biggest inspirations the world has ever received. Your life can bring about a change, a revolution. You can be one of the biggest names on this planet. You can be and have anything you desire. You can do it, I promise! Just affirm to yourself '*I can*.' Stand in front of the mirror, look yourself in the eye, and say it aloud '*I can* do it!' or '*I can* shake up the world' and feel the power rush!

Enthusiasm is Viral

> *Enthusiasm is the mother of effort, and without it nothing great was ever achieved.*

– Ralph Waldo Emerson
(1803–1882, Essayist, poet, and transcendentalist)

The word 'enthusiasm' is derived from '*en*' which means in or within and '*theos*' which means God. It means having God within or being one with God. Every religion in the world talks about displaying enthusiasm.

Children are excited about anything; they provide wonderful examples of enthusiasm and like children, enthusiastic people radiate strong positive energy. When you are enthusiastic, you will develop the ability to radiate positive energy that will turn heads wherever you go. You develop charisma that sparks off you. Enthusiasm makes you curious and seeks more from life. It will develop interest in you to learn and grow. Your enthusiasm will get you hooked on, build momentum, and affect you and those around you. It will light up your life making even the most trivial thing delightful.

> *The great accomplishments of man have resulted from the transmission of ideas and enthusiasm.*
>
> – **Thomas John Watson**
> (1874–1956, Industrialist)

But you can only be enthusiastic about what you love, about the things that you believe in and when you do what you love and believe in, your journey becomes enjoyable. Only then will you keep your focus and keep going. Only then can it battle fear and worry. Only then can it overcome stress. Only then can it develop the ability to persuade, and only then can it encourage action and help you be more successful.

Enthusiasm best arises out of something we love. What is it that you love? Draw enthusiasm from there and spread it across your life.

Enthusiasm doesn't let you dwell on difficulties and rather helps keep you pushing on. Enthusiasm is the vital key to move from thoughts to action. And where enthusiasm exists, procrastination disappears, problems vanish, and negativity doesn't appear. Without enthusiasm, success happens only in your dreams.

Success and You

What is success? The definition of success changes from person to person. But what you achieve after being successful is not as important as what you become after being successful. Hence, it is fair to say that success is not in things or events, but in you. Success is not what you achieve, it is what you become.

If you work purely for the sake of money, you may know what it is to be successfully happy. But you will never know what it is to be happily successful. Instead, when your work becomes one of self-expression, money comes in search of you as a natural by-product.

Many people are caught in the vicious circle of have-do-be. They want to *have* money so they can *do* business, so that they can *be* successful. They want to be successful so they can make money. But they can't make money because they don't have money. And because they don't have money, they can't start their business and ultimately can't become successful. They are trapped in this vicious circle. There is only struggle here. Only when we realize that we have to adapt the system of be-do-have. We don't get what we want. We only get what we become. If you want to make money, you have to work like a businessman. And to do the work like a businessman, you need to think and act like a businessman. Hence, be-do-have.

Success and Happiness

Success is not the key to happiness. Happiness is the key to success. I once asked someone what would make him happy? He replied: 'I will be happy when I get a high paying job.' When he got a high paying job, I asked him 'Now that you have got your high paying job, you must be really happy, isn't it?' He replied 'No my friend, once I get a mansion for my family, then I will be happy.' After a year, he was able to buy a mansion for himself and when I asked him if he was happy, he replied 'I will be happy when I get a limousine for my family.' I am sure even after he gets his limousine, he won't be happy.

> *Happiness resides not in possessions, and not in gold, happiness dwells in the soul.*
>
> – **Democritus**
> (460 BC–370 BC, Philosopher, formulator of atomic theory for universe)

Most people wait for a right moment or a right event or a right circumstance to be happy. And at the end of their lives, they feel exhausted and see their whole life as one long struggle. Life itself means happiness; from happiness, through happiness, and to happiness.

Tathaastu!

As a child, when you asked your parents for a candy, were you ever refused? No. Your parents loved to see you happy. So, they got you a candy. In your smile, lay their happiness. Our common God is also our father and we are his children. So, if you ask him for something, he will certainly give you, for in your smile lies his happiness. But there is a concept to understand here. If you have ever noticed the posture of any God, you can see that the hand is always in a vertical position with the palm facing towards you. In the Hindu mythology, it means *Tathaastu* meaning 'So be it.' So, whatever we ask or tell God, the answer is always *Tathaastu*! If you complain about not having enough money, the answer is 'So be it!' and you always end up not having enough money. If you are happy and grateful for the money you have, no matter how small the amount, the answer will be 'So be it!' and you see your financial conditions improving. If you are just happy and grateful for the happiness in your life, the answer will be 'So be it!' and soon, you see yourself living a life happier than ever. So, whether you complain or express your gratitude, whether you ask for something trivial or massive, the answer is always 'So be it!'

Be Happy, but not Satisfied

Don't be satisfied with what 'success' means to others. Don't be satisfied with what 'satisfaction' means to others. Define what 'satisfaction' means to you.

Not being satisfied does not mean you don't have to be happy. Also, being happy does not mean that you have to be satisfied. It only implies that you appreciate and enjoy what you already have, while being focused on getting more. Does this situation sound familiar? Most of us postpone happiness until we become or achieve something. We fail to see that success is not the path to happiness but happiness is the path to success. Be happy in the here and now. You have a million reasons to be happy right now, irrespective of where you stand in your life right now. Make peace with the idea of prosperity. It is good to ask for more in life. But it is madness if you're not happy in the process of achieving it. Be happy, but not satisfied.

5

Aligning with the Source

Developing a Working System

A good system shortens the road to the goal.

– Orison Swett Marden
(1850–1924, Spiritual writer in the New Thought Movement)

Align yourself with the source and learn to work with it in a system. With a system, you can bring the balance into your life. With a system, you can amplify your energy. With a system, you can enlarge your life. If you ask any CEO the importance of working with a system, you will be amazed at what you can do with a system that works.

Every organization has a system, and the organization with the best system produces the best leaders, and the best leaders produce the best results. Make a system that works best for you. A good system shapes your culture, dispels ignorance, harmonizes your personal and professional life, keeps you focused and inspired, helps you record your performance, and gets regular feedback and guidance, whenever necessary.

Adopt a system that includes ways to align with the source. For instance:

- Reading books/listening to audio CDs
- Nurturing mind, body, and spirit
- Maintaining a journal
- Coaching/mentoring

Reading Books

A book must be an ice-axe to break the seas frozen inside our soul.

– Franz Kafka
(1883–1924, Writer)

A book can teach you so many things, but you must choose the right book. A good system is one where the inflow of knowledge never stops. Every good system has a good learning system. That is why the world's best leaders are also the world's consistent readers. They know what a book can do. They will tell you the same: today a reader, tomorrow a leader. One life is too short to make all the mistakes. By reading books, you can learn from the mistakes of all the brilliant minds that have walked on our planet.

The reading of all good books is like conversation with the finest men of the past centuries.

– Rene Descartes
(1596–1650, Philosopher and mathematician)

You never know which word, which line can unleash the Superhero in you. You never know which chapter, which page will enlighten you. You never know which paragraph will set you free. You never know which quote will give you the fire, the confidence. A book is so magical that any part of it can transform you forever. But you have to read so that you can find that magical moment.

A truly good book teaches me better than to read it. I must soon lay it down, and commence living on its hint. What I began by reading, I must finish by acting.

– Henry David Thoreau

(1817–1862, Philosopher and leading transcendentalist)

Carry a book wherever you go. You never know what the future holds. If you are stuck in traffic, while others are busy honking and complaining, you are busy being wise. When your flight is delayed, while others are busy gossiping, you are busy being enlightened. When your college is called off, while others are busy playing video games, you are busy finding solutions.

Five Things to do Everyday

- Smile
- Appreciate
- Encourage
- Never criticize
- Make people feel they are great

We now live in a world where social structure has become more important than ever before. Relationships are everything. And if you take care of your relationships, everything else takes care on its own. There won't be any business problems, there won't be any communal problems, there won't be any war, there won't be jealousy, and there won't be hatred, all because there are no people problems.

Distorted families, broken relationships, low self-esteem, and lack of motivation are on their highest levels ever. Do you know that the count of babies born has dropped? People are so stressed out that the companies are coming out with schemes to offer honeymoon packages, family planning holidays, etc., to their employees.

> *Those who bring sunshine to the lives of others cannot keep it from themselves.*
>
> **– James Matthew Barrie**
> (1860–1937, Dramatist and novelist)

Smile, appreciate, encourage, never criticize, and make people feel they are great! These are the five rules for an everlasting relationship! Smile, for a person walking across the street who is going to commit suicide can see your smile and change his mind.

Appreciate people more than you can. You can let them know their pants are looking nice, the tie they're wearing is looking good, their smile is very natural, they have beautiful eyes, they did a good job, well done, you deserve it, etc. Appreciate people, and try to appreciate from your heart. Remember, what gets appreciated, gets repeated!

Encourage people to believe in their powers. Make them believe in themselves. Restore their faith in themselves. Share with them the knowledge you rediscover in this book, empower them, let them know that whenever they need a support, you'll be there for them. Encourage people to go for the best. Be a fire in someone's life.

No matter how high you rise in life, be humble. Don't boast about yourself. Go down to their position, no matter how high you are in life. And tell them that they're great. People want to be appreciated and credited. Everyone is great; if you meet someone who sweeps the street, tell him that he's great, because you simply can't sweep the street like him. He is a professional.

If you meet a person who works as a waiter in a restaurant, let him know that he's great, because you simply can't be as hospitable as him to a bunch of strangers. If you meet a soldier, let him know that he's great, because you can't be away from your family and serve your country. Everyone in this world, no matter what they do, is great. Win people's hearts and they will let you rule the world. These are the principles to a legendary living.

What's Happening?

We all need refreshments and a boost every once in a while. In the process of action, we only manage to be positive for the first couple of days. The trail of setbacks and negative feedback from the world circles us back to the initial point. So, we motivate and throw ourselves back into action. And this cycle continues. We get fired up – we throw ourselves into action – we fall back – Again we get fired up and so on. You know how it goes. Most people get so caught up in this vicious cycle of making a living that they forget living. Make the process worth it. Hence, include in your system the 'happening' day.

Every fifteen days, do something that becomes the 'happening' news in your life. It may be going on a weekend vacation, meeting an old friend or a relative, attending a motivational seminar, throwing a party for your friends, undertaking an adventurous activity, going to a spa or a parlour, joining a group meditation event, attending a religious prayer, or just going to a restaurant with family and having quality time together. It can be anything that means 'happening' to you.

> *Respond to every call that excites your spirit.*
>
> – **Rumi**
>
> (1207–1273, Theologian, poet and sufi mystic)

Look into your recreational goals. Pick out a suitable recreational goal and schedule it for the current bi-weekly Sabbath. Even God took a day off, so you can too!

You're not a machine. So, don't expect yourself to work three hundred and sixty-five days without breaks. These fortnightly recreations will, in fact, increase your productivity. You will no longer be detached from your personal life, you will not feel detached from the boundless energy in you, you will feel a sense of fulfilment, deal with stress better, boost your self-esteem, and give yourself a positive lifestyle, and much more.

You can schedule your short-term, middle-term, and long-term recreational and/or spiritual goals in sync with these fortnightly 'happening' days. Learn to live less seriously and more sincerely. Take care and nurture your mind, body, and spirit equally. All are equal. Learn to harmonize your mind, body, and spirit!

> *Activity and rest are two vital aspects of life. Finding them in each other – activity in rest and rest in activity – is the ultimate freedom.*
>
> – **Sri Sri Ravi Shankar**
> (1956–, Humanitarian, spiritual leader and ambassador of peace)

Would you drive a car without brakes? Absolutely not! Sooner or later you are sure to crash. Then how can you expect your life not to crash when you don't have breaks in it? You are not a machine. You are not a human doing, you're a human being. So just be sometimes. Don't be consumed by the daily dust of life. Don't let life take charge of you. You take charge of it.

Pressing the pause button allows life to catch up with you. We learn the important lessons of life in solitude, and by allowing time for those lessons to sink in, to be absorbed in our subconscious mind. One of the requirements of achieving success is to learn from mistakes and you can learn only when you take breaks to see them. Putting in long hours of efforts without a break can actually backfire. You can drain your brain to the point where you become ineffective and you're not even aware of it.

Even the Occupational Safety and Health Administration (OSHA) has declared stress as a hazard of the workplace, which costs the American industry more than $300 billion annually.

Be Mindful, not Mind-full

An increasing number of people are lost in a trance. I am sure you can relate to a part of our life where you are driving, and you choose to take the usual route to your destination. While driving, you get lost in a trance. You just keep driving, ignoring the route. After a while, you realize that you had to take the previous left. Or you realize that you have driven way past your destination.

In other instance, you walk across the street. An old friend of yours apparently walks down the same street, walking towards you. On seeing you, out of surprise and happiness, she waves but you are lost in a trance, ignoring everyone and walking by. After walking a distance, you remember you saw someone waving. So you turn around only to find that it was your good old friend.

Be conscious of yourself, your acts, and your situations. Be mindful, not mind-full.

Applying the pause button helps you in self-reflection, boosts creative thinking, gives you clarity, gives you self-fulfilment, and increases your productivity.

Reconnect

You can choose to reconnect with your own ancient wisdom that with each and every breath becomes more alive. By pressing pause, you get the chance to give yourself the best by trying new things – a new game, a new book, a new movie, a new recipe, or indulging in a hot bath or relaxing with some music. You can choose to soak in nature, observing the beauty in it. You can shut down your electronic devices and give yourself and your family some personal time. You can practice the attitude of gratitude. You can just live in the present or choose any other method that makes you happy and relaxed.

Scientists confirm that in order to effectively maintain your focus and keep your mental energy on higher levels, you have to pause for short periods of time. Research proves that not only is taking regular breaks from mental tasks important, but also skipping these breaks can lead to increased negative stress, and eventually exhaustion.

Successful people in every area of life have practiced the art of spending time in solitude to play with and reflect on their ideas and experiences. Some listen to music, while others daydream, meditate, or simply close their eyes. If you don't pause now, you will be forced to pause later.

Maintaining a Journal

'What difference will it make to write down the words that no one but I will see?' This one question can be your best friend or your worst enemy. Your journal offers you self reflection, holds you accountable for your own life, encourages positive thinking, gives you directions, encourages you to be honest with yourself, helps you plan effectively, inspires you to take actions, and keeps track of your growth.

A journal, however, is not just about writing, reading must follow. Constantly monitor your growth by reading your previous day's, week's or month's writing. Observe the things that help you progress, then, amplify those things.

For example, the following are the topics you can write in your journal. At the end of each day, you can update these in your journal.

1. *People I heard:* You can write the names of people who called you. Choose to write only important names if you must. You can include any important conversation you discussed.
2. *People I called:* You can write the names of people whom you called. Again, choose to write only important names if you must and you can include any important conversation that you discussed.
3. *People I met:* Mention the names of the people whom you met. If you're a person who meets hundreds of people every day, take into account only important people you

met in a day. You can include the important things they gave you or said to you.

4. *Places visited:* Include the places that you visited in a day.
5. *Vision seen and shared:* If you've added a new goal to your life, if you've had a vision that you'd like to achieve in life, mention it here.
6. *Intuition/God's message received:* If you get a gut feeling about something, write it here.
7. *Love seeds planted:* The things you did for others in a day, out of which you got no profit. For example, helping someone pickup the books they dropped, helping a blind woman cross the road, charity, etc.
8. *Blessings received:* Unexpected gifts, unexpected surprises, meeting anyone special, or receiving anything for free, or anything that you consider as a blessing, include it here.
9. *Lessons learned:* What are the lessons that you learnt in a day? Pen it down.
10. *Actions taken:* What did you act upon? What actions did you perform? It can be personal, professional, or social responsibilities. Write it down here.
11. *Favourite quote of the day:* Write the quote which inspired or made your day.
12. *Idea(s) of the day:* You've got an idea, no matter how big or small, write it down here.

Your journal is like the 'best of your life' collection, in which everything important to you is recorded. Talking about making a journal won't move a feather in your life. Make it!

Have a Mentor

> *If I have been able to achieve something, then it is by standing on the shoulders of the giants.*
>
> **– Isaac Newton**
> (1642–1727, Physicist and mathematician)

Have a mentor and be coachable. Come into contact of the people who rekindle the fire in you and push you higher, who make you go the extra mile, and who make you go for the brass ring. Find a person who inspires you, become his student and learn from him. Drink the knowledge that you thirst for.

Have a mentor with whom you can share everything. Be transparent about yourself, for only then can your relationship with him be stable. Having a mentor can speed up your journey to your goal. A mentor can help you to deal with difficult situations and rise above them, give you the experience you never had, bring out your hidden talents, notice potential in you that you might not see in yourself, and introduce you to a window of opportunities. The mentors you choose have been there, done that. So, you can learn from their ups and their downs. Even a book on the person you idolize can become your mentor, as when you become a student, the teacher eventually shows up.

When drops of rain fall in the ocean, they too become salty. But when a single drop of water enters an oyster, it becomes a pearl. Similarly, when you come in the hands of a mentor, you become more than what you thought you could be, you evolve into something greater.

Learning from the Source

Self-discipline

Self-discipline has been one of the most important lessons of my life. Soon, I came to understand that this is a case not just with me, but with most successful people. The most essential ingredient for success is the mastery of the self. It is the process of self-observation and self-control.

Every great success is a result of self-discipline. Self-discipline conditions us for success. Simple rule: Self-discipline for self-success.

The truth is that all of us are already one hundred per cent self-disciplined, but only about our existing set of habits. All of us exhibit the will power, responsibility, dedication, patience, persistence, priorities, and focus. The secret to your own success lies in your hands, not others. The key to achieving your goals is in your hands, not others.

Willpower

Know that your success requires nothing but the *very best* from you. Muster the courage to say 'no' to the petty things. Learning to say 'no' gives you the chance to say 'yes' to the big things. Indeed, no one can distract you without your permission. Refuse to compromise on your standards, refuse to be distracted.

> *Obstacles are like wild animals. They are cowards, but they will bluff you if they can. If they see you are afraid*

of them, they are liable to spring upon you; but if you look them squarely in the eye, they will slink out of sight.

– Orison Swett Marden
(1850–1924, Spiritual writer in the New Thought Movement)

An employee must have the willpower to say 'no' to unnecessary leaves. An entrepreneur must have the willpower to say 'no' to the unethical offers from clients and competitors. And you must have the willpower to say 'no' to the unimportant things and people in your life.

Have a vision, take an oath and give it everything you've got!

Responsibilities

God has entrusted me with myself.

– Epictetus
(55 AD–135 AD, Sage and philosopher)

Don't be afraid to take charge. Sometimes, you put on your best game when you least expect it. Since childhood, I was a very shy, introverted, and a reserved person. I had a fear of talking to strangers. I did not prefer much of travelling since I would have to use public transportation that would, in turn, introduce me to a whole bunch of strangers. And unlike any other day at my school, this day was different. I had to deliver an oratory speech in front of my 65 classmates. The worst part, it lasted for about 10 minutes and it was a compulsory exercise as part of our exams. So I couldn't even skip it. I only hoped that I didn't faint on the podium. I hesitatingly went up to the podium with a fake smile on my face, hiding my fear. Looking at the wall behind the class and not looking the faces sitting in the class, I completed my speech. I can tell you it was such a sense of relief! On that particular day of every week, a movie is screened in the auditorium. To my surprise, it was cancelled on that day. Instead, four teachers who taught four different batches of students of the same grade came forward with a brilliant idea. They had planned for an oratory competition, which meant that a student from each batch had to deliver an oratory speech, only now in front of 260 students. The brightest students for the other three batches completed their oratory speech. And here I was, sitting in the last row of the auditorium, having fun with friends. Neither was I the brightest in studies, nor was I my teacher's favourite. So the odds were in my favour. It was time for the brightest student from our batch to make his teacher proud. To everybody's astonishment, not one but the top ten of the brightest students of my batch refused to comply with our teacher's request. Finally, our teacher understood that nobody would want to do it if requested. Little did I notice that the teacher stood right next to me. He looked at me and said: 'You are going on that stage.' And I said 'me … ah ah me? Umm … No, not me'. He replied, 'If you don't go up on that stage, I am going to kick you fella!' All 260 eyes were on me. Without any option, I stood up and started walking towards the stage. My teacher called out my name and said, 'Dilip, You can do it. I believe in you.' I went on that stage and to my shock there was no wall behind the auditorium this time. What was I thinking? The auditorium was at an inclined angle so wherever I looked, I saw faces. I took a moment and then I started, only to realize after a minute that I mixed up the speeches. I started again from the beginning. This time around, I looked at the faces, moved around the stage and completed my speech successfully. And by the time I walked back to my seat, I was a different person altogether. I had lost my fear of talking to strangers. I was no longer the shy, introverted, and reserved guy. Just because I undertook a responsibility, no matter how much I despised it. Little did I know that I would go on to address gatherings of thousands in attendance.

Take up responsibility, it will either bring out your talents or you will no longer be given responsibilities. That's all that can happen.

Dedication

> *Only one who devotes himself to a cause with his whole strength and soul can be a true master. For this reason mastery demands all of a person.*
>
> **– Albert Einstein**
>
> (1879–1955, Nobel Prize-winning physicist)

Nothing big in life happens without dedication. Personal and professional life, they both require dedication. If you've got a dream, then you've got to be honest and loyal to it. Stop dedicating precious time of your life to matters and issues that hold you back, that prevent you from being the best you can and living your dream.

When you are dedicated to an oath, a vision, and a mission in your life, priorities become clear and action becomes untiring. Someone rightly said that discipline is just choosing between what you want *now* and what you want *most.*

Patience

> *Adopt the pace of nature: her secret is patience.*
>
> – **Ralph Waldo Emerson**
> (1803–1882, Essayist, poet, and transcendentalist)

Leaders are patient beyond human limits. A seed takes years to produce fruits. But meanwhile, you have to nurture it with appropriate quantity of water and sunlight. Similarly, success requires patience. Concentrate all your thoughts upon the work at hand. This means being able to put the unimportant and unnecessary things and people aside and focus on enjoying your way to your goal. Little by little, you *will* travel far!

> *For all things difficult to acquire, the intelligent man works with perseverance.*
>
> – **Lao Tzu**
> (604 BC–531 BC, Founder of philosophical Taoism)

Every Superhero perseveres. Some persevere for their relationships, some for their employment, and some for their education. Some others persevere in prayer, some persevere in good work, and some persevere in the service of God. But we all persevere, one way or the other. All we have to do is align our perseverance in accordance with our goals.

Persistence

Go back to your childhood for a minute and you won't need my guidance on persistence. As a child, we were persistent on getting that exact same chocolate, getting that exact colour balloon, going over to our friend's home to play, etc. When you're not ready to give up, you'll eventually get what you're looking for. The rock is broken by the last stroke, but that does not mean the previous strokes were useless. Success is a result of continuous efforts, despite all odds. Don't stop on the journey, but keep going.

> *Energy and persistence conquer all things.*
>
> – **Benjamin Franklin**
> (1706–1790, Inventor, politician,
> and the founding father of the United States)

Choices

When you are self-disciplined, tough choices become easier and decisions become clearer. You become single-minded about your decision and you won't have regrets about it. Our life is the sum total of the choices we make. Our choices in life will make life what it is. And every choice we make takes us forward or pulls us backward.

We become the choices we make.

– Anonymous

And even though we know what the right choice is, unless we are self-disciplined, it is highly unlikely that we make it. The right choice might be a path full of stones and thorns, with ups and downs, and probably you will have to walk it alone. You will be responsible for the choice and will have no one to blame. It will require dedicated focus and action, will power, patience, perseverance, and persistence which only self-discipline can provide.

Time Management

Time is measurable, finite because there is a limit to what your body can do. Five hours remains five hours in clock time. If you want more time, you have to contract the deadline to complete the task. Deadlines can be stretched, not time.

Why is it that we find sitting in front of the TV so inherently relaxing? Why is it that we find ourselves gossiping for so long? Why do we take our time for granted? Why does our sense of necessity weaken and fade away without considerable effort?

You must always be mindful to cut off the flow of useless information and progressively move in the direction of your dreams. Develop the principle of doing things when you need to do and you'll have time to do the things what you want to do, when you want to do. Protect your time - invest it, don't spend it. For each second that you kill, you lose two seconds - One from the present and other from the future.

Use a scheduler to manage your time wisely and effectively.

> *Let not thy winged days be spent in vain.*
>
> – **A.P.J. Abdul Kalam**
> (1931–2015, 11th President of India,
> *aka* the People's president)

You will never learn to manage time if you limit the things that you want to do in life. The context and relevance of time can only be defined based on what you want out of life. Also, no change will come about, if you just believe what is said. It is meant to be practiced. Even if everything happens on time and yet what happens in that time is not beneficial and worthwhile, then it is mere clock management. Time management is an attitude towards life. Your life is the sum of your seconds. Spending away seconds today is spending away a part of your tomorrow. Remember this.

We are blessed with time for constructive and creative purposes. Time lost is life lost. Be a wise master of your time and you will be a wise master of your life.

The Five-minute Buster

> *The future is something which everyone reaches at the rate of 60 minutes an hour, whatever he does, whoever he is.*
>
> – C.S. Lewis
>
> (1898–1963, Novelist, medievalist, and essayist)

Several years ago I had a board meeting to attend. Although there were only five of us, I couldn't make it on time as my previous appointment extended beyond its deadline. By the time I joined the board meeting, I was already five minutes late. And I can never forget what one of the board members said. He said, 'You're not late by five minutes. You've postponed your success by five minutes. It's all about the mindset.' It was a total eye opener for me.

Remember, time and age never take a U-turn. So, make the most while you have it. There is no going back. Invest it to get the utmost in health, happiness, and success! Practice accountability – be punctual, with yourself and with others. Those five minutes forever changed my view towards time. We must not only believe in the adage 'time and tide wait for none' but also act upon it. You fix a purpose to every penny that you have, but you do not do that with your time. Time encapsulates all opportunities. Yet our seconds turn into minutes, minutes turn into hours, and hours into days and all run into drain. Unplanned living is the surest way to kill time. Every hour and every minute of your life must be determined for a purpose, eventually leading to a more fulfilled life. Use time wisely and leave your footprints on the sands of time.

No Excuses Please

Excuses arise out of fear, from lack of interest, from lack of knowledge, from past experiences, and from judgments and moods.

We made an excuse because we feared it may result in an unpleasant situations, we made excuses because it did not interest us, we made excuses because we did not have adequate information about something, we made excuses based on our past experiences, and we made excuses based on our personal judgments and moods. Anything that we do repeatedly becomes a habit. Soon enough, it becomes an unconscious action. We start giving excuses without our conscious consent and by doing so, we miss out on the opportunities we encounter. If your excuses arise out of fear, it is only appropriate that you act. We now know that activity and activity alone cures fears.

If you know your passion and purpose, you will no longer need to do anything that does not excite you. You only have to do what interests you.

If your excuses arise out of lack of knowledge, forge ahead and act. You will learn more by doing than just gathering information. Still, if your undertaking requires some expertise, gain knowledge. It makes no sense to make excuses and run away.

If your excuses arise out of past experiences, know that you are not in control of your past, but you're still in command of your future. As we discussed earlier, don't be pushed by your fears, be led by your dreams.

If your excuses arise out of personal judgments and moods, just *be.* After all you're a human *be*ing and not a human *do*ing. Take a break, meditate, listen to some soft music, and don't let your personal judgments and moods blind you from seeing the truth. And then, go ahead and stretch yourself beyond the illusion of your limitations!

Realize that more excuses you make, the less you learn. And the less you learn, the more stagnant your life becomes. Life is growth and learning is essential for that to happen and action is essential to learning.

You can make either money or excuses, but never both. You're either a part of the problem or part of the solution of your own life. There is no in-between.

> *Don't do what you'll have to find an excuse for.*
>
> **– Anonymous**

The problem is not that we don't know anything. The problem is that we know everything and yet we do nothing about it. You know that you can do it, and you can do it exceptionally well. We've discussed this. Now, the question isn't 'can you?' it's 'will you?'

Stop making excuses and start making history!

Work Hard to Get It, Harder to Keep It

Work hard to get it, harder to keep it! You work hard to get good and then work harder to get better. It's hard to get on top. But the work you have to do to get to the top is only part of the work you have to do to stay on top.

Your Anchors

Your anchors help you in setting a grand trajectory in life. Anchors are the primary values your life stands for. What are the core values that are essential to you? How often has it happened that even when we have very few things in our to-do list, we fail to get them done? This is because we have not defined the anchors in our life. Your anchors can provide you stability and strength in both worst and best phases of your life. Some of your anchors can be:

- Daily progress
- Be cheerful always
- Harmonious relationships
- Financial freedom
- Never give up

Once you've set the anchors for your life, introspecting with respect to your anchors will help you understand yourself and your actions better. Clarify your goals and check to see if they are in sync with your anchors.

You must be wide awake and alert to the challenges of life, for he who takes his eye off the path will surely tumble. Without a clear vision of your own, you can be easily distracted. But having strong anchors in life will prevent you from slipping into distraction. Even if you slip away into distraction, you will not feel good and it will help you bounce back on track with a richer experience.

7

Connecting Yourself with the Source

Introspect More than Extrospect

The philosophy of the wisest man that ever existed is mainly derived from the act of introspection.

– William Godwin
(1756–1836, Journalist and philosopher)

What is the kind of conversation you are having with yourself? Are you playing to win or are you playing not to lose? How high is your self-esteem? Who or what is your influence? Are you reacting instead of responding? How have your perceptions changed? And what caused the change?

Do you know what your next goal is? Is success a onetime affair to you? Are you feeling good being a lucky-by-chance success victim? Or is it that you have realized where you have slipped and are now ready to take control of your future? If yes, then let there be nothing more important than to renew your belief system, to go from goal to goal, from happiness through happiness, play to keep winning, and do not let what held you back hold you back any further.

What is Your Relationship Status?

Look well into thyself; there is a source of strength which will always spring up if thou wilt always look there.

– Marcus Aurelius
(121 AD–180 AD, Roman emperor)

Your first relationship has to be with yourself. You must have a very clear relationship with yourself, knowing why you feel the way you do, or why you think in a particular way. The first step is to be aware of your own self.

Do you know with whom you talk the most in your life? With yourself! Some scientists claim that talking to yourself might be the highest form of intelligence.

But, do you have a relationship with yourself? If yes, what is your relationship status with yourself? Do you love yourself? Or, is your inner soul your best friend?

From the moment we wake up in the morning till we go to sleep at night, we think, worry, wonder, and have conversations with our self. And the harsh reality is that most people's self-talk is rather brutal. People constantly ask themselves the wrong type of questions. They beat themselves up or occasionally find themselves in total denial of reality. Unfortunately, it is estimated that the average person's self-talk is between 60% and 85% negative, where the subject is only thinking about what he or she doesn't want.

The conversations we have with ourselves run at an incredibly fast speed, perhaps 10 to 20 times faster than what we speak out loud. The average person can say around 500 words per minute. But our internal thinking, our self-talk, runs many times faster than we can talk out loud.

Our inner conversations also have a powerful impact on our emotional well-being and motivation. Becoming aware of what we are saying to ourselves about ourselves can help us understand why we react the way we do to events and people in our life.

Do you make a list of things you don't need from the supermarket? Of course not! However, when you think about what you don't want in your life (let's say you don't want bad health, you don't want to be in poor financial crisis, etc.), then it is exactly as ridiculous as making a list of things you don't want from the supermarket. Remember, we only believe what we say to ourselves. Every word you utter is an affirmation to yourself.

Love yourself, respect yourself, and compete with yourself. Pull yourself, push yourself, question yourself, and answer yourself.

Use Winning Words

Words are also actions, and actions are a kind of words.

– Ralph Waldo Emerson
(1803–1882, Essayist, poet and transcendentalist)

Practice Intentional Speech

Even in your conversations, use great words. Use words that fill you up with energy and excitement. Use words that describe who you truly are. No matter how fake it may sound initially, as with all matters, with time you will find it truer than ever. Do it intentionally.

Remove inferior and ordinary words like good, normal, okay,

mediocre, need, can't, impossible, problems, difficulties, unfortunately, ego, etc., from your vocabulary and replace them with great, legendary, impeccable, etc.

Use words like successful, trustworthy, strong, focused, diligent, and team player to describe yourself. Replace the negative beliefs you hold about yourself with positive words and clichés. To remind yourself, make a list or a bookmark with the words you have to use every day.

I Am the Greatest

When I think of self-esteem, I think of one name unanimous to it. I think of Muhammad Ali.

> *Be not afraid of greatness: some are born great, some achieve greatness, and some have greatness thrust upon them.*
>
> – **William Shakespeare**
> (1564–1616, Poet, playwright, and dramatist)

Even before entering the ring, he asserted to himself, 'I am the greatest.' He saw himself as a champion and that's why he became a champion even inside the ring. It does not matter what others think of you, it does not matter how others see you, the only thing that matters is how you see yourself.

What is your worth? How do you see yourself? When you see yourself in the mirror, do you see a happily successful entrepreneur, or a government employee, or a professional, or a student, or a homemaker, or a perfect partner, or a good friend?

> *No matter what you think, your light cannot be dimmed by the perception of darkness.*
>
> **– Anonymous**

You are priceless. You are one gem of a person! You have such great powers within you that can change the course of the world forever. This power is in each and every cell in your body. You are made from the very heart of this power. There is no other you on this planet. You are unique. You are rare. You are a wonder of this universe. And you don't need anybody's approval for it.

We forget that how we see ourselves is how the world sees us. A cat can see itself as a lion and gain the confidence of a lion, while an amazing human being can look upon himself with doubt and disbelief like a helpless creature.

If your goal is to become a millionaire, can you stand in front of the mirror and call yourself a millionaire? Do you walk and talk like a millionaire or like a broke? This one step shows how you see yourself. I once heard an entrepreneur, still in his twenties, say 'I was always lucky because I never thought I was unlucky.' Terrific! What an attitude, remarkable self-esteem. No wonder, he has more than 100,000 people working for him.

Goodness is the Enemy of Greatness

As we discussed earlier, when you be more, you can do more. When you have more, you can share more. But, often we unconsciously begin to settle for good. Some of us may have the passion, the energy, but we lose the sight of our target. Hence it is important that we ask ourselves questions like, 'What is my target?', 'Where am I heading?', 'Am I on course?', 'What got me distracted?', 'Am I giving my best to achieve it?', 'Am I enjoying the process?' and so on.

Greatness is a birthright for every living human being. Your greatness is guaranteed without any question or negotiation. The power to dream is built in everyone at the point of conception. Remember the old adage, 'If you keep doing what you've been doing, you'll keep getting what you've always got.'

We may do many good things. But that may be precisely our problem; we are good, but not yet great. Make that shift – good to great!

Expect to Win

It's all about the right mindset. It is important to spend some time in self-reflection and set our mindset in the right direction. Ask yourself 'am I playing to win or am I playing not to lose?'

There is a world of difference between expecting to win and wanting to win. When you expect to win, you have amplified your imagination. You've set a powerful intention for yourself. On the other hand, wanting to win remains merely an aspiration, a wish.

When you play to win, you don't make excuses. You make progress instead. You set your mind on a target, you get a mental picture of it, and then you go for it.

But when you play not to lose, there are excuses, there is whining. There is no thrill of participating in greatness, and there is no excitement.

If you expect that good things will happen to you, they will. If you expect that you are going to encounter problems and eventually fail, so shall it be. The power of positive expectation can ever be underestimated.

Imagine yourself to be the 20th of 22 children, prematurely born baby girl. Your survival is doubtful. At an age of four years, you contract a double pneumonia and scarlet fever that leaves your left leg paralyzed. Doctors pronounce that you would only be able to walk with the support of a metal leg brace. But you know the expectations you've set for yourself and you believe that you can achieve anything you want to. You develop a very strong expectation from yourself to be able to walk without braces and you believe in it. You begin visualizing and feeling the excitement of being able to walk without braces. Now you begin performing your rudimentary exercises to strengthen your left leg. At the age of nine, you are able to get rid of the metal leg brace and by age 12 you have developed a rhythmic walk, which doctors say is a miracle. That same year you decide to become a runner. You enter a race but you come in last. For the next few years every race you enter, you come in last. Everyone discourages you but you are determined to become an Olympic runner. You persevere and one day you actually win a race. And then another, until you've won every race you entered.

Eventually you, who were told that you would never walk again, went to win three Olympic gold medals. This is what Wilma Rudolph did. Wilma Rudolph is an inspiring example of positive self-expectations, which gave birth to the courage, determination, and belief to succeed and fulfil the expectations she had from herself.

Winners expect to win in advance because they know that life is a self-fulfilling prophecy. So never get into anything expecting to lose. Go expecting to win. Introspect every now and then and set your sails in the right direction.

Don't Just Win, Keep Winning

> *Don't take rest after your first victory because if you fail in second, more lips are waiting to say that your first victory was just luck.*
>
> **– Anonymous**

Attitude of Winning

Your attitude to win is more important than the facts required to win. Only the right attitude can empower you and only when you are empowered, you can be bigger than your challenges.

Whether it involves competing at work or competing every four years in the Olympics, winning brings advantages that make it easier to keep winning. Winning provides an aura that makes everything seem to glow. Winning helps you in *self-determination*. Winning more gives you more control over your destiny.

Look at the finest Superhero souls in every field. They keep winning. Winning isn't a onetime affair to them. So don't bask in success with your eyes closed, keep your eyes wide open, unlike most people who bask in their success with eyes closed only to find themselves back at the bottom. Celebrate the victory and keep moving. That's how you'll go down in glory. That's how you'll make yourself a legend. And that's how you'll live on in the hearts and minds of people. And no matter how many victories you have to your credit, say to yourselves and to the world, 'This is just the beginning!'

Who Is Your Influence?

Show me your friends and I'll tell you who you are.

– **Mahatma Gandhi**
(1869–1948, Father of the nation)

Born to Fly, Doomed to the Ground

Professor Samuel Langley was doomed to the ground when he let the opinion of others into his soul. The people you surround yourself with have this effect on you, whether you accept or not, whether you believe it or not, whether you realize it or not. But they do. Remember: what influences you, makes you. You become your influence.

If you want to soar like an eagle, associate yourself with an eagle. If you associate with achievers, you will become one. If you associate with thinkers, you will become one. If you associate with givers, you will become one. If you associate with complainers, you will become one. So the big question is this: who is your association? Who is your influence?

Respond, Don't React

> *We are disturbed not by things, but by the view which we take of them.*
>
> **– Epictetus**
> (55 AD–135 AD, Sage and philosopher)

Happiness has less to do with circumstances than with our own attitude towards life. Happiness does not happen to us, it happens by us. Each of us is the creator of our own thoughts and state of mind. This does not mean ignoring the often painful reality of what happens, but understanding that you can choose to respond, rather than react to it. You can choose your response to anything at any given moment. In any given situation, no matter what our senses tell us, we have choices. We don't always recognize it, but we have choices.

> *The possibilities are numerous once we decide to act and not react.*
>
> **– George Bernard Shaw**
> (1856–1950, Playwright)

You can choose to be tired and furious with the demands and pressure of a hectic day. You can feel miserable about bad relationships, your colleagues, or the weather. Or, you can stop and breathe calmly for a few moments, finding some beauty to focus on, something to be grateful for in all the clutter. You can choose between forever complaining on a rough childhood, or focus on healing and moving on, for happiness needs to be cultivated, and not a thing to be achieved.

But blaming others for your misery, even if partially true, can only give you excuses and not the happiness you crave inside. Happiness, at its core, is about discovering meaning and counting your blessings, not your woes.

Build emotional resilience and exercise emotional self-control. If you can't control yourself, you won't be able to control the events and situations. It is the self-control which makes every control possible. Getting quality sleep at night, investing time in personal growth, maintaining a healthy diet and exercise routine, turning off your mobile phones and Wi-Fi connectivity for a while, maintaining a healthy work-life balance, etc., will help you build your emotional resilience. A simple way to build emotional resilience is to practice silence and be grateful for all that you can.

Reaction arises from negativity while response arises from positivity. When you respond, you're in control. But when you react, you lose control. In your response, you have a chance to express your emotions in a way that feels satisfying

The word 'thank you' alone has the potential to change the course of your life. Listing out all the things you feel grateful for is a therapeutic exercise that is sure to chase away the nost persistent blues.

ometimes, we may not realize how much we're relying on hers to get things done. It is okay if you can't rise to the top thout the help of others. Nobody can be a self-made man woman but saying 'please' to everyone when asking for is good manners and a very important principle. When ise the word '*please*,' it shows respect and consideration e effort another person puts forth to help us and is also verful way to establish rapport, build relationships, and op your own character. Your consistent use of '*please*' is thing that will most definitely help you stand out in a who are mindful or mindless to the words they use in ily life.

en it comes to apologizing for our mistakes, instead ng with rage or feeling annoyed and irritated about ion, take the simple approach – just humble yourself u're sorry. At first, the water may be cold, but then ed to it and you're glad you did it. The more you elf to swallow your pride, be vulnerable, and give pology, the easier it will get. Even when it's not saying sorry won't do you any harm. But it can e situation.

mple thing to say, 'I'm sorry' when an apology is today parents are shocked and frustrated when

to you and clearly communicate your feelings for the others. You have a chance to act with authenticity and integrity, and ultimately to act in a way that you can feel good about later.

Ego

Many people succeed in life in terms of money and fame but they cannot maintain a good relation with others because of their ego. They feel that they have reached the pinnacle of success and soon consider others inferior. When there are ego issues between husband and wife, there is no peace in the family. In some families, because of the ego issues between husband and wife, they would be quarrelling all the time. Many marriages end in divorce and their children suffer, due to the ego of parents.

Best friends often part due to ego. Ego does not encourage you to make your enemies your friends. Ego does not understand the feelings and concerns of others. It just comments. It waits for its turn to speak. Ego expects to be praised by all, in the family and at the workplace. If it didn't get what it expects, it bursts. Ego at the work place stops growth. If you are a preferred employee by your boss, you should not feel that you are very great and treat others at a low level. Ego knows no peace. It constantly worries and doubts. To attain peace, we need to let go of the ego and live in the present.

Ego causes many miseries in life. The egoist person invites troubles and if he doesn't get the attention he needs, he starts developing all sorts of grudges against others. The egoist person sees everything with a magnifying glass and often finds fault with others.

Ego lacks a sense of oneness. The love of the ego is conditional; it gives only in expectation of receiving something in return.

The ego wants to be right all the time, it loves conflict, it loves to spot the 'otherness' of the other person, and it creates a space for jealousy, anger, hate, and misery. The ego has no kindness and it cannot share. The ego loves competition and comparison and creates stress and misery.

When we are egoistic, we miss out on many learning opportunities through which we might otherwise grow. Ego simply stands for Easy to Get Out!

Win with Love

Getting success and fame are really good. But, we should learn to accept these calmly, shredding our ego. There is no need to boast of your achievements. Because if you are successful, you really don't have to explain, your results and accolades will speak for themselves.

Awareness about others is very important. Every person in this world directly or indirectly plays a role in your life, whether you believe it or not. Where ego divides, love unites. While ego commands the mind, love wins the heart of others. Try every day to pull ego back in just a little, just for a

moment and look at the situation or the person, thro
eyes of love.

How to Reduce Ego?

1. Don't rely on your physical appearance to im
   use your religion or spirituality practices to
   are not here in this world to impress or pl
   don't even try.
2. Be aware of false modesty, and don't se
   of others. If you think you are a winner
   don't need anybody's approval of it. Gi
   attention that you don't need to se
   others.
3. Don't speak badly of yourself and
4. *Love:* It is what will protect you a
   ego. Where there is pure love, eg

Thank You, Please, and Sorr

I can no other answer make,

(1564–1616, P

The word 'thank you,' due t
lost its essence – the heart
Gratitude has an incred
forces like love, compass
life. True thanksgivin
gratitude.

their child refuses to offer apologies when the situation calls for it.

These three words – thank you, please, and sorry can build understanding, love, and compassion in any relationship when used.

Be an Approachable Person

One of the important factors in any relationship is to be approachable. Be an approachable person, whom people like talking to, listening to, and being around.

No matter how rough a day you had at work, drop that baggage at work before coming home. Most people return with the baggage of frustration from office to home and often, a very trivial or sometimes an unnecessary event is enough to take out the frustration. Reaction becomes the response. Don't bring your professional matters home and don't take personal matters to work. There is a thin line between personal and professional life that you need to acknowledge and set balance.

People like to approach and communicate with someone who makes them feel safe to speak up, who doesn't keep all the attention on himself and encourages others to voice their opinions. How would you feel if someone you are talking to isn't listening to you at all? And if he isn't listening to you, he is with utmost certainty not understanding you. Instead he is already thinking what he must speak when you pause.

Would you like talking to him or approaching him ever again? Now reverse the roles. Would anyone like to talk to you or approach you ever again? So learn to stop, listen, and understand. People don't want someone who will always give them solutions. People want someone who will be with them, listen and understand.

Be honest. Why do you tell a lie? What will happen if you tell the truth? People will get hurt, upset, and not understand you. But are you here in this world to please people? Do you have enough time in your life to make everyone understand your point? No! And you definitely can't make everyone in this world happy. So, all you have to do is speak the truth and move on. The ones who will understand will come with you, the others won't. That's all. You get to see who walks with you temporarily and who walks with you permanently. Speaking a lie can do more harm to you than to those whom you lie to. Be open, be honest, remember that whatever you do, including a lie, can spread in all areas of your life and ultimately become a habit.

Most relations fade because of improper communication. Therefore, it is very important to understand that our communication with others has very little to do with *what* we say, and more to do with *how* we say it. Pay attention to how you communicate and learn from how others are communicating with you.

Follow the 'Five things to do everyday' program (smile, encourage, appreciate, never criticize, make people feel like to you and clearly communicate your feelings for the others. You have a chance to act with authenticity and integrity, and ultimately to act in a way that you can feel good about later.

Ego

Many people succeed in life in terms of money and fame but they cannot maintain a good relation with others because of their ego. They feel that they have reached the pinnacle of success and soon consider others inferior. When there are ego issues between husband and wife, there is no peace in the family. In some families, because of the ego issues between husband and wife, they would be quarrelling all the time. Many marriages end in divorce and their children suffer, due to the ego of parents.

Best friends often part due to ego. Ego does not encourage you to make your enemies your friends. Ego does not understand the feelings and concerns of others. It just comments. It waits for its turn to speak. Ego expects to be praised by all, in the family and at the workplace. If it didn't get what it expects, it bursts. Ego at the work place stops growth. If you are a preferred employee by your boss, you should not feel that you are very great and treat others at a low level. Ego knows no peace. It constantly worries and doubts. To attain peace, we need to let go of the ego and live in the present.

Ego causes many miseries in life. The egoist person invites troubles and if he doesn't get the attention he needs, he starts developing all sorts of grudges against others. The egoist person sees everything with a magnifying glass and often finds fault with others.

Ego lacks a sense of oneness. The love of the ego is conditional; it gives only in expectation of receiving something in return.

The ego wants to be right all the time, it loves conflict, it loves to spot the 'otherness' of the other person, and it creates a space for jealousy, anger, hate, and misery. The ego has no kindness and it cannot share. The ego loves competition and comparison and creates stress and misery.

When we are egoistic, we miss out on many learning opportunities through which we might otherwise grow. Ego simply stands for Easy to Get Out!

Win with Love

Getting success and fame are really good. But, we should learn to accept these calmly, shredding our ego. There is no need to boast of your achievements. Because if you are successful, you really don't have to explain, your results and accolades will speak for themselves.

Awareness about others is very important. Every person in this world directly or indirectly plays a role in your life, whether you believe it or not. Where ego divides, love unites. While ego commands the mind, love wins the heart of others. Try every day to pull ego back in just a little, just for a

The word 'thank you' alone has the potential to change the course of your life. Listing out all the things you feel grateful for is a therapeutic exercise that is sure to chase away the most persistent blues.

Sometimes, we may not realize how much we're relying on others to get things done. It is okay if you can't rise to the top without the help of others. Nobody can be a self-made man or woman but saying 'please' to everyone when asking for help is good manners and a very important principle. When we use the word '*please,*' it shows respect and consideration for the effort another person puts forth to help us and is also a powerful way to establish rapport, build relationships, and develop your own character. Your consistent use of '*please*' is a little thing that will most definitely help you stand out in a crowd who are mindful or mindless to the words they use in their daily life.

And when it comes to apologizing for our mistakes, instead of burning with rage or feeling annoyed and irritated about the situation, take the simple approach – just humble yourself and say you're sorry. At first, the water may be cold, but then you get used to it and you're glad you did it. The more you train yourself to swallow your pride, be vulnerable, and give a genuine apology, the easier it will get. Even when it's not your fault, saying sorry won't do you any harm. But it can lighten up the situation.

It is such a simple thing to say, 'I'm sorry' when an apology is called for, but today parents are shocked and frustrated when moment and look at the situation or the person, through the eyes of love.

How to Reduce Ego?

1. Don't rely on your physical appearance to impress. Don't use your religion or spirituality practices to impress. You are not here in this world to impress or please others. So don't even try.
2. Be aware of false modesty, and don't seek the validation of others. If you think you are a winner, you are one. You don't need anybody's approval of it. Give yourself enough attention that you don't need to seek the attention of others.
3. Don't speak badly of yourself and others.
4. *Love:* It is what will protect you and see you through, not ego. Where there is pure love, ego cannot exist.

Thank You, Please, and Sorry

I can no other answer make, but, thanks, and thanks.

– William Shakespeare
(1564–1616, Poet, playwright, and dramatist)

The word 'thank you,' due to its mechanical repetition, has lost its essence – the heartfelt gratitude it seeks to express. Gratitude has an incredible potential to release positive forces like love, compassion, joy, and faith in an individual's life. True thanksgiving arises out of appreciation and gratitude.

they are great) and master the art of communication, you'll turn into an amazing person.

Revisit Your Lists

As you grow in your life, and as you begin to introspect, it so happens that some of our new experiences add value to our lives. Nonetheless, it becomes important to review our lists.

Revisit your 'why' list. Write the new motivations, reasons, and purposes behind your goals.

Revisit your 'goal' list and add the new goals that you've set for yourself. If some goals require modification, do it.

Revisit your 'fear' list, and if you have taken action, you can see some of your fears have turned into your strengths. If all of your fears have been eliminated, you can remove those pages from your diary, crush them and discard them into the dustbin. Feel the joy when you crush your fears!

One of the most important things to do in your diary is to see that you grow your dreams, not fears!

Revisit your system. If your system requires modification, do it by yourself if you can or else you can consult your mentor and make a modified system.

If you have made an 'idea' list, see the progress that you've made so far. What are the ideas you've worked upon until now. If you have new ideas, include them. If you have made growth on an idea, tick that and write your achievement.

Your diary helps you sail in the right direction, make the right action plans, gives you strength and purpose in life, and helps you in self-motivation. It tells you how much action you have taken to accomplish your goals.

In order to make this practice a habit, it is very essential that you spend at least fifteen minutes a day with your diary. It is not just your diary; it's your legacy. Nurture it, nourish it, and watch it unfold.

8

Connecting the World with the Source

Serve

When we talk about working for a cause, we immediately get images of working for a non-profit organization. But it doesn't really matter whether it's a non-profit organization or not. A cause remains the fundamental cornerstone even for a profit-making company. The reason of existence for a company to be in business is the cause to be of service to others.

The most successful organizations – they serve us with their products and services. Top artists – they serve us with their stunning art. Great sportsmen and sportswomen – they serve us with their amazing performances in the game.

Master chefs – they serve us with their impeccable culinary skills. Every Superhero serves. Every business is about serving. Every employee serves the company he works for. Every good university, good hospital, good government aims to serve the people. A good king is a servant of his people, because he serves them. The one, who serves more, wins more.

> *It is one of the most beautiful compensations of this life that no person can sincerely try to help another without helping him or herself. Serve and you shall be served. If you love and serve people, you cannot, by any hiding or stratagem, escape the remuneration.*
>
> – **Ralph Waldo Emerson**
> (1803–1882, Essayist, poet, and transcendentalist)

It is the nature of the universe. The stars and moons serve us by delighting us. The clouds shower rains and serve us by helping irrigation for agricultural growth. The trees grow and serve us with their beautiful flowers and fruits; they serve other birds and animals in building their habitat. Even the sand serves us in making glass. Nothing in this universe goes un-served. No man can be as selfish as deciding not to serve others. It is not possible not to serve others. Even if a man decides not to buy vegetables and fruits from the market and decided to grow them in his backyard, he must sow the seeds and when the seeds grow into trees, they serve as a shelter for other birds and animals. So again, he ends up serving. The seeds are carried away by the wind and result in pollination. Soon, plants and trees grow in other places serving more birds and animals, even though he decided to sow the seeds in his backyard by deciding not to serve. No matter if he is an employee or an entrepreneur, he serves others. No matter if he is awake or asleep, he is serving others. Despite all his actions, man ends up serving. Every act, no matter how small or big, follows a chain reaction of service.

No job is just a job, but a calling. When was the last time your heart sang at work? When was the last time you considered your work as a chance to serve? Do you think of your work as a calling, that your work matters and it delivers impact to the world?

When you pursue a genuine cause, love what you do and

do what you love, you get up in the morning, energized, and look forward to the day's work. And when the world applauds you for your service, it is because of the impact you have made, which no one can ever take away from you. This simple step can create wonders – Serve, Serve, and Serve.

Give Back to the World

You will rise by lifting others.

– Robert G. Ingersoll
(1833–1899, American political leader)

The world gives us so much, along with the people in it. Sadly, most of us take this for granted. Nobody in this world is self-made. The entire world and everyone and everything in it are interconnected. So many people and things have assisted you to get here in your life. So, it is only befitting that when you have more than what you need, you assist others in becoming what they want to become.

You can give to the world from wherever you are, with no matter how much you have. Anyone can make a difference, even a little five-year-old. You just have to find what you can do and then do it. You can contribute in any way possible. The world needs contributors, no matter how small. The world would be in anarchy if it had only consumers and no producers.

Plant a Love Seed Each Day

Every religion in the world tells us to show love and sow a random act of kindness. Your acts of kindness are the 'love seeds' – the one who will bear the fruits is you. Plant a love seed each day and know that in each seed is the promise of a forest. Planting a love seed each day can truly be a life-enriching experience that almost immediately fills your heart with a joy like none.

> *The hand cannot reach higher than does the heart.*
>
> – **Orison Swett Marden**
> (1850–1924, Spiritual writer in the New Thought Movement)

Sandy, one of my good friends, happens to be an entrepreneur; a profession he fondly chose at a very young age. 'Entrepreneurship is a lifestyle' he could be heard tell, more often than he would utter his own name. About three years into his business operations, Sandy seemed to have hit the road's end. Despite his boldest plans and hard labor, there seemed to be no light at the end of the tunnel. He was exhausted. He barely made any profits. One day I learned that after crossing the point of exhaustion, he took a break from his business to be with his family. Sandy's grandmother, who was in her 80s at the time, always dreamt of visiting a world-famous temple on the banks of river Yamuna. When Sandy became aware of this he immediately decided to fulfil his grandmother's most desired dream. Perhaps even her last. He made a few calls and arranged for their pilgrimage. Surprised by her grandson's gesture, the grandmother was moved to tears. She went on her last pilgrimage, her most special and treasured one. Her life seemed complete the day she set foot inside the temple; she was immersed in a sheer state of bliss and gave thanks. This was a love seed Sandy had planted for his grandma. His only motive – fulfil his grandmother's final dream. That was it. Upon their return Sandy decided to give his business another chance. He labored day and night; and this is where the miracle happened. Within 2 weeks of Sandy planting his love seed, his business revived and went on to generate 10 million US dollars. But what could possibly explain such an anomaly? Sandy had the power of planting love seeds. On different levels, we all experience what Sandy experienced. We all have our different versions of miracles, different stories of blessings, and different experiences with luck. Call yourself fortunate, lucky or blessed – on a deeper level it is all the same.

By planting a love seed you will not only be making the community happier and the world a better place for someone, but also be placing yourself in their hearts. A love seed a day keeps blessings coming all the way.

Call the outcome what you may, but I urge you, do not credit it to fate. We are observers but for a very short period of time. We only get to see about 70 of the billions of years this planet has seen. So, isn't life too short to consider yourself victim of fate?

Your Blessings Can Do What Your Efforts Cannot

> *Reflect upon your present blessings - of which every man has many - not on your past misfortunes, of which all men have some.*
>
> **- Charles Dickens**
> (1812–1870, Writer)

It happens often that we put in the right effort and in some cases, we put in the extra effort only to see little or no improvement at all. It is not that the rewards are not coming. It is just that we are not tuned in to receive them yet.

For example, take the radio waves. There are radio waves all around. It doesn't matter where you are, the radio waves are there. But just because you can't perceive them with your five senses, doesn't mean they are not present. When you first hear a station is not when the station started broadcasting. The signals were present and the station was broadcasting even before you tuned in. But only when you tuned in your radio set, you started receiving.

Now, what would you do if your radio set went silent suddenly and none of the stations came in? You know that the station is already broadcasting. Others, who might have already tuned in, might be receiving the signals and being broadcasted since the time they tuned in. So you'd know that your receiver is the problem and you'd check *your receiver.*

Ninety nine percent of the time, the issue is with your receiver and not the transmitter.

So you see when you work hard and still results don't come in, it is time to check your receiver. It's like that radio wave and the signal is already being broadcasted. If you aren't seeing the picture, it's not God/Universe who isn't transmitting but it is your receiver that isn't working right. And one way to tune in and set your receiver right is to feel happy and count your blessings. Some scientists recommend counting your blessings twice a day, every day.

One of the most effective ways to count your blessings is to be grateful for all that you have. You can be grateful while you're walking, while you're seeing a beautiful flower, while listening to a beautiful piece of music, when you're with your loved ones, etc. There is no limit to the things you can be grateful for.

First be grateful to all that you already have. You can be grateful for the things, events, circumstances, and people in your life. You can also include the things that happened in a day that you're grateful for. From there, remind yourself of the things that you want to achieve. And through gratitude, bring them into existence.

Practicing this attitude of gratitude and counting your blessings can do for you what your efforts earlier could not. Pure magic happens when we count our blessings. One flicker of light in a dark cave dispels the darkness!

9

Being the Source

Change

The end of life is to be like God, and the soul following God will be like Him.

– Socrates
(469 BC–399 BC, Philosopher)

You can't change anybody's life until and unless they are willing to change theirs. Change yourself and then change the lives of others. Else, others are going to change you anyway.

If *you* want to succeed, *you* must change. First change and you shall be successful. Because there is no guarantee that you will change after you become successful.

Change with Time

With time, times change. Many companies that ruled a century ago are obsolete today. Why? They did not change with time. Even organizations today have realized that to stay in the game, they must constantly change themselves as well as their products and services. If they are not updated, they are outdated. Change is an ongoing process, from birth until death. Change is constant. If you don't choose to change positively, you'll automatically change negatively.

To improve is to change; to be perfect is to change often.

– Winston Churchill
(1874–1965, Politician and former UK prime minister)

Success is directly proportional to change. The more you

change, the more you succeed. It is easy to sit at home and watch movies but difficult to write your journal. It is easy to gossip but difficult to introspect. It is easy to sleep for half a day but difficult to wake up early and work on your goals. It is easy to talk of doing but difficult to quit talking and start doing. The more you change, the more you succeed. Change requires daily grinding.

Change is a process, not a single step. Change of habits, change of mindset, change of character, change of health, change of perception – all are individual processes.

It's like learning how to drive a car, or speak a new language. Deciding today to learn driving doesn't mean that you'll wake up and drive tomorrow. Deciding today to learn French doesn't mean that you'll wake up and speak in French tomorrow. The most important thing to know is that you can use techniques and practices to change yourself.

You are always in the process of change. Hence, setting your thoughts right, setting the right goals, planning the right activities, and regular introspection can bring about drastic changes in you.

The process of change is no different from the process of achieving goals.

1. The big 'Why': Why do you want to change? What is driving force behind your change?
2. Follow your passion to get in the direction in which you must change.

3. Defining the junction: Change is a process. It never has any destination. It only moves from one junction to another. So, change always exists. All you have to do is to define your junctions. What do you want to change first? From there on, what do you want to change next? Define your junctions, so you know where you are heading.
4. Gain the knowledge required to change. Be aware of what actions you will have to take.
5. Act/Replace limiting beliefs: Once you have gained the knowledge, jump into action. Action must be done both mentally and physically.
6. Ask For feedback/help: Get regular feedback from your mentor. Don't feel embarrassed or shy to ask for help. It only means that you're still open to learning and are not egoistic.

Change of Habit

A habit is a choice that we make at some point, and then stop thinking about it, but continue doing the same thing. A habit can be changed by making meaningful choices. Make your choices carefully. For example, once you learn to quit, it becomes a habit. If habits make or break us, how do we change our habits?

Change starts with the acknowledgment that no matter what the habit is, it can be changed. The process of changing the habit is the same as the process of change. However, you must also identify what is causing the habit and what motivated it to occur. With every improvement you make towards changing the habit, you can reward yourself so as to stay motivated in the process. Change might not be fast or easy. But with time and effort, change is possible.

Be a Messenger of Love and Happiness

> *I dare to open my heart more to the wonders that I hold inside myself without fear.*
>
> **– Anonymous**

As adults, we have become abnormal. We have lost our way and relationship with life! This is where returning to our child-like nature can make a difference. It is about seeing life as an adventure and rediscovering joy in the little things. It is about daring to enter hitherto uncharted territory. It is about the thrill of the journey itself and no longer about reaching the destination. Develop a child-like wonder. You will find wonder only when you're open to finding and experiencing it. You will find wonder when you look at reality with its beauty as well as its flaws, and knowing that it is deep, precious, and meaningful.

Learn to involve yourself completely in whatever you do, feel the essence of doing it. Then you will experience wonder. There is no limit to the things that can awaken wonder in you. A starry night sky, tiny wildflowers hidden in the grass, the sound of flowing water, the fresh smell of mud when it rains, the touch of a loved one, a piece of music, etc.

But you can hardly be delighted or experience wonder when you treat things, events, and situations indifferently. You'll never feel wonder if you're always in a hurry. If you are not happy with yourself, you cannot be happy with others. If you cannot love yourself, how can you love others? When you are too busy, you will fail to notice the real blessings in your life. And in the grip of indifference, you wouldn't care less. 'So what?' becomes your response instead of 'Oh wow!'

Wonder is when you rejoice in the play of your senses: smell, sight, touch, taste, and sound. Wonder is changing from saying 'so what' to 'Oh wow!'

Love Without Limits

You are a storehouse of love. All the love you seek is within yourself. From the very point of your inception, you were love. Love is your natural state of being. Love yourself, for unless you love yourself, you can't love anyone or anything else. Only when we seek love within us, can we affect the world outside us.

We use the words 'I love you,' referring to our dream partner, our dream house, our dream car, etc., but when was the last time we told ourselves, 'I love you?' Your body silently performs all its functions so you can enjoy the very best. When was the last time you recognized it with the magic words 'I love you?' Today, tell yourself '*I love you*!'

Power of Relationships

> *If you have it, Love, you don't need to have anything else, and if you don't have it, it doesn't matter much what else you have.*
>
> – **James Matthew Barrie**
> (1860–1937, Dramatist and novelist)

When your relationships work, your personal, professional, and spiritual worlds work. When your relationships don't work, nothing works out for you. Nurture your relationships with love. Be in a relationship where there is love. You don't have to necessarily befriend somebody for social or political concern. Once you choose to love someone, don't judge them. If you judge, you will have no time to love them. Whoever you are, wherever you are, take care of your relationships and everything else will take care on its own. Whatever the situation, be love and with love. Always!

Go to your soulmate, hold their hands, and tell them how much they mean to you and how much you love them. Sings songs for them, buy them flowers, take them out, express your love, show how deeply grateful you are for having that person in your life. Learn to set your relationships in right direction in life.

Your love is limitless. It can outshine the stars and the moons. It can make the world go round. It connects you to your natural state of being.

Make Your Inner Self Larger than Life

The majority of the people in this world are really concerned about their lives. But only a minority of us is concerned about our legacy. What good is a life when you don't build a legacy to leave behind? It's not just our lives in our hands, but also our legacy. Every day, every step you take, you create your history and every path you take leaves your legacy. But to create a legacy, you don't wait for the right path or the right door to show up. You make your own path, your own doorway and walk right through it. But what kind of doorway are you going to create to walk through? After you have created your doorway, and when you walk through that door, stand for what you believe in and let your passion illuminate the path.

Live in the Present

> *Every morning we are born again. What we do today is what matters most.*
>
> – **Buddha**
> (563 BC–483 BC, Founder of Buddhism)

Setting goals or developing a vision of the future is powerful. But the execution of the goal depends on what we do in the present moment. The more we are present, the better the quality of our doing will be.

Science tells us that the present moment is the only thing where there is no time. It is the point between past and future.

It is always there and it is the only point we can access in time. Everything that happens, it happens in the present moment. Everything that ever happened and will ever happen can only happen in the present moment. It is impossible for anything to exist outside of it.

When you live in the present, you are living where life is happening; you're living where all the beautiful and stunning creations happen. When you live in the present moment, you have escaped from the sufferings of the past and anxiety of the future; you experience performance benefits, health and relationship benefits, peace of mind, and a complete life. In a way, living in the present allows you to be a larger version of yourself.

Some of the points that you can include in your beliefs are the following:

- Today, I will listen to my soul.
- Today, I will be insanely great at what I do.
- Today, I will flirt with my ideas.
- Today, I will take a chance.
- Today, I will do something that I have never done before.
- Today, I will not complain.
- Today, I will be grateful for all that I can.
- Today, I will listen to more than I speak.
- Today, I will appreciate and encourage others.
- Today, I will laugh till it hurts.
- Today, I will take care of my body.
- Today, I will have a fantastic day.

There is only one time that is important – Now! It is the most important time because it is the only time that we have any power.

– Leo Tolstoy
(1828–1910, Writer)

How are You?

What is your usual reply when somebody asks you 'How are you?'

Do you put a big smile on your face, sparkle in your eyes and gratitude in your heart and say 'I am fantastic', 'I am doing great', 'I am on top of my game', 'I am awesome', or do you just casually say 'I am okay', 'I am good', 'just fine', etc.

Look at a newborn. Within a few days, it starts smiling on seeing a recognizable face. The child smiles and laughs on seeing a toy or the moon or the vehicles passing by. A child smiles 400 to 500 times a day and when we grow into adults, the number of smiles per day comes down drastically.

Next time somebody asks you how are you? With joy on your face and sparkle in your eyes, say, 'I am fantastic!' You literally have plenty of reasons to be.

Let YOU be the Light

Most of the time, we are caught up in the problems of the moment, trying to fix them for short-term benefit.

Some people ignore their problems and keep wondering why the same problem shows up every time. Some people get attached to the problem and end up being a part of the problem. Some people enjoy the problems and keep wishing for more problems to show up. Then, there are those people who simply make themselves into a solution. This is the kind of person you should strive to be. Make yourself a solution. Make yourself a key to the lock. Every company, every influence is either making you a problem or a solution.

Don't be the one that consumes. Be the one that produces. Don't be the one that watches things happen. Be the one that makes them possible. Don't be the one that puts limits on others. Be the one that removes all limits from yourself and others. Don't be the one that gets jealous. Be the one that gets inspired. Don't be the one to avoid responsibility. Be the one to take it up. Don't be the one to see problems. Be the one to see possibilities. Don't be the one to say, 'this is not my job.' Be the one to say, 'let me help you.' Don't be the one to say, 'darkness will soon pervade over light.' Be the one to say, 'my light will forever outshine the darkness.'

> *There are two kinds of light – the glow that illumines, and the glare that obscures.*
>
> – **James Thurber**
> (1894–1961, Cartoonist)

Light up the bulb within so you can illuminate the world. If you are looking for an external light source, you will always remain a beggar. Unless the source of light becomes you, you will always be at somebody else's mercy. You will always feel inadequate. Change yourself and be an inspiration to the world. Only when you are illuminated, can you illumine your surroundings. Only when you are illuminated, can you show the path to those who are in the dark. Don't seek light in others. Let YOU be the light!

The Dream Merchant

> *A man sooner or later discovers that he is the master-gardener of his soul, the director of his life.*
>
> **– James Allen**
> (1864–1912, Philosopher)

We discussed in the beginning of the book that your life only becomes as great as your purpose. Here I remind you again, only goals are achieved and set again, but purpose is lived throughout. Make your purpose great and you'll achieve the golden goals that anyone has ever seen.

Don't stop setting goals no matter how many you've achieved. As we discussed earlier, make 500 goals in your life and when you've achieved those goals, set another 5000. The first 500 were only a practice. Now the real game begins!

Protect your goals. Don't let the hustle of the city deter you from your path. Introspect, have a meaningful conversation with yourself, relax and unwind, and give yourself the best of everything.

Learn like a student, teach like a teacher, become the domain expert, and never give up. Build your castle of dreams with the stones that critics throw at you.

Practice, perfect yourself, do what is right, build a solid leadership pipeline, bury the hatchet, make peace, work harder, be of service to others, mentor somebody, and bring them up to your position.

Ask for more, use the power of '*and*,' don't settle for mediocre when great *and* greater is possible.

Be outstanding, exceptional, remarkable, and legendary. Settle for nothing, but true greatness.

Dream without fear, love without limits, and let your life sing its song.

Be the Superhero, be the dream and the dream merchant!

This is It!

> *That is what learning is. You suddenly understand something you've understood all your life, but in a new way.*
>
> – **Doris Lessing**
> (1919–2013, Nobel Prize-winning writer)

In the beginning of this book, I promised you that I wouldn't be teaching anything that you didn't already know. And now that there is a twinkling flame woken in you, protect it and grow it. It has always been your destiny.

Just as every seed has in itself the power to become a forest, you have in yourself a source of infinite power. Find that source and take in that power. Use this power to create anything your heart wills. Explore, pray, laugh, enjoy, push harder, and celebrate each moment. Life is a blessing in itself and let your life be a blessing to the world.

> *You're braver than you believe, and stronger than you seem, and smarter than you think.*
>
> **– A.A. Milne**
> (1882–1956, Writer)

You have to put something in to get something out. Everything you want and need is in your reach. Define what success is to you, then go be it. Make your own path. Think crazily, even if others laugh at you. Act bravely, even if you are all alone. Believe in yourself. Carve a niche, and get out of mediocre standards. Collect experiences and ignore doubters. Never stop learning, and look at your goals every day. Never stop being grateful, no matter what happens. Refuse to lose, refuse to be defeated, refuse to be cheated, and refuse to have regrets.

Believe that anything is possible. See possibility when others see impossibility, take risks, be focused, feel the abundant holy support, embrace your childlike wonder, be curious, and contribute your awesomeness.

Do what you want to, speak what you feel like; you are not

here to suit people's perceptions about you. You are here to be you and fulfil your purpose. Trust your instincts, be fearless, be kind to everyone including yourself, and stay away from negativity as much as possible.

Feel great about yourself because you are. There are so many reasons for you to be exceptional and legendary. You have such powers in you that can surprise even you at times. You can make anything possible. There is no limit to what you can do, be, or have. You can create any opportunities you desire. You can turn around any situation with your will and action. You can live a life to its absolute perfection, and this is the truth. This is your time, the time you've been waiting for all this while.

> *There can be no failure to a man who has not lost his courage, his character, his self respect, or his self-confidence. He is still a King.*
>
> – **Orison Swett Marden**
> (1850–1924, Spiritual writer in the New Thought Movement)

The Proverbial Second Chance

> *Here I stand now, with a sweet tingling feeling all over, recalling the last time I was here, and I am glad that I am here again, while wondering why I didn't recognize it earlier. But now I have got the chance to recognize and deal with it more effectively and I know that I can*

visit this place as many times as I want, and take as many chances as I want, because I finally realize that I, am in total control of my life.

– Dilip Bathija

At some point in our lives, we've all wished that we could go back in time, correct our mistakes, and grab the countless opportunities we missed. We wish that we could go back in time with our heads full of knowledge, belts busting with experience, and go do it all over again. The proverbial second chance is something we've all wished for.

I told you earlier that no matter what your age is, no matter what colour you are, no matter where you're from, no matter what , you can be successful, you can standout and you can live your dream. Now, what if I told you that you could have a proverbial second chance to do it?

You can avoid the mistakes you previously made. You can build on the successes you previously enjoyed. You can nurture the positive relationships and avoid the bad. You can stop being affected by criticism and opinions of others. You can tap into your wealth of experience during times of indecision. You can always know when and where your time and money should be spent.

You can bury the hatchet. You can dream big. You can gain the willpower to persevere amid all odds. You can gain the strength and wisdom to take another chance and dare to dare. You can practice what you preach. You can learn to see the silver lining. You can use every word with love and compassion. You can feel good about yourself and make peace with yourself. You can love beyond measure. You can change yourself. You can be the best in the world. You can be the light the world needs and you can change the world!

You can be your own boss. You can lead a world-class organization. You can attain personal and professional greatness. You can live your life to its fullest. You can be a jet setter. You can be a guru. You can be anything you want. You can be you, the real Superhero.

And as others wish for the proverbial second chance, remind yourself that if, and only if you choose so, every moment is a chance to write your destiny, for your life after all is your self-fulfilling prophecy.

Now rise from the ashes and become the phoenix. Let your glory and wisdom keep blazing on forever. This is your chance. This is your time. Remake your life into something truly spectacular.

My love, support, and cheers to you – the Superhero soul!